CREATING AN EFFECTIVE BUSINESS PLAN

The Easyway

Michael Lane

Editor: Roger Sproston

Easyway Guides

Easyway Guides

© Straightforward Co Ltd 2022

All rights reserved. This book may not be copied in any way, either in a retrieval system, or electronic or mechanical copying without the permission of the copyright holder. A British Library Cataloguing in Publication data record is available from the British Library.

978-1-80236-057-8

Printed by 4edge Ltd www.4edge.co.uk
Cover design by BW Studio Derby

The information in this book is correct at the time of going to press. The author and publisher have no liability for errors or omissions contained within or for any changes in the law since publication.

CREATING AN EFFECTIVE BUSINESS PLAN

CONTENTS

Introduction

SECTION 1-WHAT IS A BUSINESS PLAN?

Chapter 1. The Purpose of a Business Plan	**17**
What is a business plan?	17
How long must a business plan be?	19
What resources do you need to produce a business plan?	20
Key points from Chapter One	21
Chapter 2. Ten Quick Tips When Writing Your Plan	**23**
Writing your plan for the reader	23

SECTION 2. SETTING OUT OBJECTIVES AND STRUCTURE/LOCATION OF YOUR BUSINESS

Chapter 3. Setting out Clear Objectives for Your Business and Defining a Business Strategy	**27**
SMART Criteria	27
Mission statements	28
Defining your Business Strategy	29
Strategic analysis	30
PESTE Analysis	30
Political	30
Economic	30

Social	31
Technological	31
Environmental	31
Auditing resources	31
Physical resources	32
Human resources	32
Financial resources	32
Evaluation of future options	32
Strategic implementation	33
Planning and allocation of resources	34
The Structure of a business	34
Management of people and systems in a business	34
Business control systems	35
Strategic threats	35
Key points from Chapter Three	37
Chapter 4. Choosing The Structure of Your Business	**39**
The sole or proprietary business	39
Partnerships	39
The Limited Liability Company	40
Looking at Franchises	41
Advantages of a franchise	41
The disadvantages	42
Different types of franchise	42
Patents and registered designs	44
Patents	44
Registered designs	45
Trademarks	45
Service marks	45

Copyright	45
Key points from Chapter Four	46

Chapter 5. Location/Premises/Employees-Making the Right Choice — 47

Location of your business	47
Working from home	48
Planning permission	49
Change of use	49
Health and safety at work	50
Inspectors	50
Employing people	51
What are my responsibilities as an employer?	51
National Insurance Contributions	52
Discrimination and the Law	52
Trade unions	52
Tax and national Insurance-more details	52
The law and you as an employer	54
Recruiting and motivating employees-doing it yourself	55
Job centres and employment agencies	55
Training	55
The personal approach	55
Key points from Chapter Five	57

SECTION THREE. MARKETING AND PRICING STRATEGIES

Chapter 6. Marketing Your Business — 61

Market research	61
Marketing generally	64

Advertising	65
Leaflets	65
Directories	66
Advertising in magazines	67
Newspaper advertising	67
Television advertising	67
Radio advertising	67
Using an agent	68
Direct mail	68
Using sales representatives	68
Online marketing	69
Search engine optimisation	70
Making your site visible to search engines	70
Quality content	70
The use of key words and phrases	71
Search engine marketing	71
Purchasing traffic	73
Email marketing	74
Affiliation	74
Using vouchers and coupons	75
Co-registration	76
Social media	75
Blogging	75
Market places (ebay etc)	77
Key points from chapter Six	79
Chapter 7. Pricing Your Product-Creating a pricing Plan	**81**
Pricing your product	81
Your costs	81

Example	82
Competitors prices	83
Key points from Chapter Seven	85

SECTION 4. FINANCIAL CONTROL

Chapter 8. Raising finance — 89
Investment of own funds	89
Short-term finance	90
Trade credit	90
Factoring	90
Invoice discounting	90
Long-term finance	91
Business loans	91
Hire purchase and leasing	91
Finance leasing	92
Operating leases	92
Contract hire	92
Soft loans	93
Grants	93
Crowd Funding and Peer-to-Peer lending	95
Key points from Chapter Eight	98

Chapter 9. Exercising Financial Control — 99
Profit and loss forecasting	99
Cashflow forecast	99
Preparing a forecast	100
Other Terms	100
Over trading	101

Collecting money on time	101
Check customer's ability to pay	101
Set out terms of trading	102
Set up a system	102
Keep clear and accurate records	102
Collect your payment on time	102
What information must be kept?	103
The advantages of a bookkeeping system for a business	104
How to record the information you need	105
Proprietary systems	105
The analysed cash book system	106
The double entry system	108
Computerised systems	109
Key points from Chapter Nine	110

SECTION 5. ONLINE BUSINESSES-ADDITIONAL CONSIDERATIONS

Chapter 10. Online Businesses	**113**
Online v traditional business	114
The technical side	114
The legal aspects of an online business	115
Business operations, supply chain and how you distribute your goods	115
The managing of customer expectations and relationships	116
Setting up Your Business Online	116
Choosing a web developer	118
Experience	118

Development skills and knowledge	118
References from other clients	119
Future project management	119
Payment methods over the web	119
The process of ordering	120
Ensure that the A-Z process is simple	121
Supplying Goods and Services-The Supply Chain	121
Setting up your business and supplying goods and services	121
Local suppliers	121
Buying from abroad	122
Choosing a supplier of goods	123
Managing the suppliers	123
Organising payment terms	123
Breaking off relationships with a supplier	124
Stock control	124
Bar code printer	125
Bar code scanners	125
Stock management systems	125
Invoicing customers	125
The storage of stock	126
Picking and packing stock	127
Delivery of items	127
Returns	128
Chapter 11. Creating Your Business Plan-Finer Points	**129**
Constructing the Plan	130
Main considerations	130
Presentation	130

Chapter 12-Example Business Plan Template 133

Chapter 13-Tips when buying an Existing Business 147
Inspecting a Business for sale 147
Goodwill 148
The process of purchasing a business 149

Conclusion
Useful addresses
Index

****

INTRODUCTION

The latest in the series of publications in the Easyway Guides series, Creating an Effective Business Plan, Revised Edition, aims to give the reader a clear and concise introduction to all the various aspects of effective business planning.

This is without doubt a very turbulent time. **Writing in 2022**, following BREXIT, the Pandemic, and now global problems exacerbated by the war in Ukraine, we also have a period of high inflation, increasing business costs such as rising interest rates, and the price of energy and rising staff costs. Moreover, we now have the supply chain problems created by all the above.

It is obvious that in the light of these crucial factors, effective business planning is vital, particularly as there are a record number of businesses collapsing. In addition, the increased success of many online businesses that happened during the pandemic is now showing signs of slowing as people slowly go back to the high street. We will be discussing additional factors related to setting up online businesses in chapter eight.

Many businesses have a hybrid model that on the one hand is underpinned by traditional methods of selling, and on the other an online sales platform. However, it is those businesses with an online only platform that will need to be very careful and pay attention to future trends when putting together their business plan.

Based on what is happening, it is very important at this time to ensure that you have a firm idea of the fundamentals of business planning to ensure that your business can get off the ground and be successful in the future. As such, this book has been produced with a view to providing the reader with a practical understanding of what is involved in the process of business planning, whether your business is traditional or an internet-based business. It is targeted at those individuals and organizations that have little experience of business planning but would benefit from an understanding of these processes. Organizations which will benefit will on the one hand include sole traders, partnerships, small companies, and voluntary organizations, and on the other hand students of business studies and economics.

The book includes invaluable information on setting up a business, employment law, marketing, and finance. There are several more recent methods (and more turbulent) ways of obtaining finance for business, such as crowdfunding and peer-to-peer lending which have been in the eye of the storm and are facing stiffer regulation.

There is also a newer method is financing by internet giants such as Amazon and Paypal. In terms of Amazon funding, a business would need to be trading successfully on Amazon and then would be offered loans, or would apply for a loan, to expand their business. Typically, the current interest rate is 6%. However, whatever method of trading or funding, to create the business in the first place you need to have followed a plan.

A model (basic) business plan is included at the end of this book which will help in the initial stages of business growth. You might find it useful to visit either www.bplans.co.uk or www.business-plans.co.uk both of which offer a range of different business plans for a wide variety of business. These will help you to tailor your plan to the business that you have in mind.

The government has also put together model business plans which can be accessed on their site https://www.gov.uk/write-

Introduction

business-plan. The whole process of business planning involves thinking and asking questions, and it is to these questions we now turn. Although most people who are faced with the prospect of producing a business plan, often in response to a request from their bank manager, feel daunted, the process is straightforward and with the aid of this book the task should be that much simpler.

****

SECTION 1

WHAT IS A BUSINESS PLAN?

- Defining a Business Plan

- Tips on writing a Business Plan

Ch.1

THE PURPOSE OF A BUSINESS PLAN

What is a business plan?

When answering this question, it is tempting to say that a business plan is simply a document which the budding entrepreneur can present to his or her bank manager, or prospective funder, as a means of assuring them of the viability of the proposed business, thereby securing start up funding.

In a sense, this is true. Banks are usually reluctant to finance small business start-ups, simply because so many have gone bust over the last ten years. Moreover, they have done so, according to many economic commentators, precisely because such small businesses have not thought about how it is they are going to survive and prosper in what is almost always a very competitive environment; they have not produced a business plan that demonstrates that they are aware of the wider business environment.

It is erroneous to see a business plan as simply a tool for negotiation with the bank manager. A business plan is, above all, a strategic document that assists the entrepreneur to think very carefully about all the aspects of the business that they are getting involved in. A good business plan will illustrate detailed research and evidence around such aspects of business as:

- The product/service; what exactly is it? It may be obvious to you, but unless you spell it out it may not be clear to your customers.
- The market; is there evidence of demand for your goods and services? Is the competition fierce? Are you entering a niche market? Is the market prone to fluctuation for any reason? If so, how do you propose to deal with this?
- Your unique selling point (usp); what is it that makes your goods and services better than those of your competitors? Price? Quality? Anything else?
- Yourself; have you got what it takes to be successful in your line of business? What relevant experience/training have you had? How do you propose to remedy any shortcomings in these respects?
- Business development; what sort of life span are you putting on the business? What are your ultimate business objectives? Growth? Diversification?
- Capital funding; what level of funding, if any, do you need to start up your own business? How much money can you afford to put into it?
- Management and personnel; are you intending to employ other people? If so, what will their roles be? How will they relate to you? Are you aware of the legal and cost implications of employing staff?
- Legal requirements; is your proposed business subject to certain legal requirements, e.g., health and safety legislation, fire regulations, VAT, licensing etc.

- Location and premises; from where do you propose to run your business? Does location matter? What size of premises do you need and what do they cost? Is it feasible and/or desirable to work from home?
- Budgeting; what are your overheads and likely level of income? Is there any scope for price variation to cope with increased competition?
- Cash flow; at what points in the year will you face big bills? When can you expect an upturn in sales? What level of overdraft, if any, will you need to service the business?

These are the key questions that any good business plan will address, and it is the process of answering them-and thinking about them-that is most beneficial to the entrepreneur.

How long must a business plan be?

There are no golden rules regarding the length of a business plan. Always, the most important aspect of the plan is the quality of research, evidence and information provided. However, if a business plan purports to cover a long period of time, 10, 20, 30 years for example-it will inevitably entail the provision of more information, thus elongating the size of the document.

Large businesses sometimes have business plans which cover a period of up to 30 years. Small businesses, if they have a business plan, normally cover a period of 2-3 years. In the case of new businesses, it is sometimes a good idea to have a business plan for the first year of trading only, to "test the water" and to review the plan at the end of the first year, producing what might be a more realistic 2–3-year plan, based on the experiences of the first year.

As a rule of thumb, however, a business plan should aim to be around 10-12 sides of paper in length, with relevant appendices attached (cash flow forecast, profit and loss forecast, budget calculations etc)

What resources do you need to produce a business plan?

Large companies producing 20–30-year business plans employ highly qualified accountants and financial experts with highly sophisticated computer equipment to assist them in the drafting of their business plans. Therefore, the small independent trader may feel somewhat ill qualified to produce such a plan. However, it is possible to produce a business plan without expensive equipment and expert advice. Because the proposed business is small, there are less complications which experts would normally deal with.

A business plan can be produced by a small trader if he/she has the following resources and assets:

- time
- commitment
- numeracy
- literacy
- patience

These are all the human resources required to produce a business plan. The only other things needed are a pen and piece of paper!

Now read the key points from Chapter 1.

****

Key Points from Chapter 1

- A Business plan is a strategic document that assists the businessperson to think very clearly and carefully about all aspects of the business they are involved in, or getting involved in.

- A good business plan will illustrate detailed research and evidence around all aspects of business.

- A good business plan will help you to understand your unique selling point as a business.

- There are no golden rules regarding the length of a business plan.

- A business plan can be produced by anyone with basic resources.

**

Ch. 2

Ten Quick Tips When Writing Your Plan

Before we look at setting out clear objectives for a business, there are a few pointers that should be followed when producing a plan. Many of these are covered in the following chapters.

Writing your plan for the reader
The starting point for any business plan should be the perspective of the audience. The questions that you need to ask yourself are:
- What is the purpose of the plan-is it to obtain funding, for example? An investor will need clear answers to their questions, such as will they get a return on their investment.
- Have you carried out market research-is your plan detailed enough-without this detail your plan will not clear the necessary hurdles?
- Do you understand the competition?
- Is the plan detailed enough? Business plans should ensure that the reader has enough information to make decisions on whether to fund you, or whatever it is that you are asking them to do.
- Focus on opportunity-if you are seeking investment in your business, it is very important to describe the investment opportunity. In short, why should an investor choose your business over and above others.

- Ensure that you cover all key areas in your plan-you should undertake research on what a plan should contain-books like this will go a long way to helping you. However, it does no harm to obtain as much specialist advice as possible.
- Do your sums-when you are outlining the costs involved you should pay as much attention as possible to detail. Potential investors, whoever they are, will turn away if the figures do not stack up.
- Create an executive summary-one of the most important components is the executive summary of the business plan. This is a summary of the entire business plan and is usually contained at the start of the plan. If investors like it they will read on. If not, they will pass. If there is no summary, they will probably not even consider it.
- Review the plan-once you have completed the plan have it independently reviewed. Select a person detached from the process.
- Implement the plan-a plan should always be viewed as a living document and contain specifics regarding dates, deadlines, and specific responsibilities.

Now turn to Section 2.

****

SECTION 2

SETTING OUT YOUR OBJECTIVES AND COMPANY STRUCTURE/LOCATION

- Setting Out Clear Objectives

- Defining Your Strategy

- Deciding on The Structure and Location of your Company

Chapter 3

Setting out Clear Objectives for your Business and Defining a Business Strategy

Before we look at the variables that should be entered into a business plan, we should look generally at the management of a business. In this chapter we will look at the process of setting objectives for a business, i.e., what are your aims and goals. We will also look at the development of a business strategy.

It is essential to have a crystal-clear idea of what the main objectives for your business are. Business objectives relate to a business as a whole and to what you want to achieve in the long and short term. Short-term objectives will relate to what you want to achieve on an annual basis, over a period of twelve months. Long-term objectives relate to a period (usually) of five years.

It has become commonplace now to set up a criterion against which you can measure the effectiveness of your business objectives. This is known as 'SMART' criteria. Within SMART all the objectives that you set for your business must be:

- Specific
- Measurable
- Agreed
- Realistic
- Timed

The above is self-explanatory and enable a business owner to set clear objectives which can be re-evaluated over time. SMART objectives should be set against a clear MISSION Statement.

Mission statements

The best way to quantify business statements is through a mission statement. The mission statement is really a vision statement that details the whole point of your business. There are four key components of a mission statement that must be succinct and clear:

- The role or contribution that a business makes-what exactly are you in business for?
- A definition of the business-this should be given in terms of the benefits you provide or the needs that you satisfy. It should not define what you do or what you make.
- An outline of your distinctive competencies-the factors that differentiate your business from the competition. These are the skills and capabilities that are offered by you as opposed to other business in the same field
- The indications for the future-what the business will do in the future, what it can realistically achieve.

A clear and coherent mission statement is written in two parts. In the first part you will outline the industry that you are in and the products that you offer. The second part comprises the business strategies that you will follow to achieve success.

A few examples might be:

- We will provide a first-class service to all customers
- We will achieve high productivity levels through sound planning, organization, and teamwork
- We will generate sufficient profits to ensure ongoing investment in the business
- We will earn high employee loyalty and motivation by respecting their capabilities and their motivation and providing training opportunities
- We will gain recognition in the market for being a highly professional, ethical, quality assured business.

Obviously, the above needs to be fleshed out and thought through but it is the basis upon which the operations of your business will be founded and on which the SMART objectives will integrate to ensure that the business moves forward and achieves its goals.

Mission statements need to be re-evaluated on a regular basis as there is always the ever-present danger that it will become just a form of words that sounds good but has no bearing.

Taking SMART objectives and Mission Statements further, basic marketing objectives should mesh with both. We will be looking at marketing later in the book.

Defining your business strategy

As the owner of your business, or one of the owners, you will be responsible for defining business strategy. Strategic management, essentially, has three components:

- Analysis-where are you now and where do you want to be?
- Choice-what options are available to you?
- Implementation-implement your strategy based on the analysis and options.

Strategic analysis

There are two distinct areas of any business that require analysis:

- The environment
- The resources of the business

PESTE analysis

There are several factors in the environment that can have an impact on your business. The PESTE analysis enables you to focus on these. PESTE stands for:

- P = Political
- E = Economic
- S = Social
- T = Technological
- E = Environment

Political

When examining the effect of political forces on a business we are really referring to legislation that has a direct impact on business, such as health and safety legislation and employment law. It is necessary to comply with all legislation and to be seen to be doing so.

Economic

Economic forces will include all the variables that may have an effect of the profitability and sustainability of your business. These can include, inflation, interest rates and, if you trade abroad, interest rates in those countries. Changes in the budget will also, invariably, influence you.

Social

Social forces can be complex and include demographic changes that will affect your business. For example, if you sell shoes, the fact that there is a falling birth rate in a particular part of the country may affect demand, will affect demand, for the type and size of shoes needed over the longer term.

Technological

The rapid changes in information technology and relevance to all businesses must be considered when devising future strategy.

Environmental

The impact of business on the environment must be evaluated and considered when formulating any business strategy.

Auditing resources

Having considered the business environment through PESTE, we should now look at auditing the resources of the business. If the business is new, then an analysis of what resources might be required to achieve your aims will be necessary. There are three main headings under which your resources will fall:

- Physical resources
- Human resources
- Financial resources

Physical resources

Physical resources include plant, machines, tool, vehicles and so on. An audit of these resources whether existing or needed in the future will include longevity, cost of future replacement and maintenance.

Human resources

This will be an assessment of staff needed in the future, if you are a new business, or existing staff if you are established. An audit of human resources should consider staff development, which will be based on the future skills requirements of staff allied to your own strategy for the business. We will look at staff later in the book.

Financial resources

This area, like the other two, is of vital importance. Without financial stability the business will not survive. An audit of financial resources will include all the sources of finance that you have. This audit will also include an analysis of debtors and creditors. The result should be a clear determination of current and future viability and, if problems are identified, the rectification of these problems.

Evaluation of future options

The next step in the process, after completing the analysis of your business, is the evaluation of all the different options that have been thrown up. This evaluation must be alongside the business goals and objectives previously set. Generally, when assessing options, there will be four available:

- Consider withdrawing from the market completely
- Consolidate the existing position within the market
- Increase market penetration
- Introduce new products or services.

The above will clearly emerge following your analysis of the business. Withdrawing from the market can mean liquidation or sale of the business. Consolidation is usually an internal process where the business may concentrate on overall efficiency. Increased market penetration essentially means expanding into new markets for existing products and services. Introduction of new products and services can mean adapting the existing technology or products to suit new markets.

Strategic implementation
There are two aspects of implementation that you need to consider. One is planning carefully the other is the actual implementation. There are three key areas into which you can break down the implementation process:

- Planning and allocation of resources
- The structure of the business
- Management of the people and the systems in the business.

Planning and allocation of resources

The resources of a business, as we have seen, are physical, human, and financial. For a new business it should be easy to plan what resources are needed and then allocate them. However, this is more complex for a growing business. The planning of physical and human resources will be easier than the planning of financial resources. We will look at financial forecasting later in the book.

The structure of a business

Again, if the business is new the structure is likely to be less complicated than a growing business. Initially, in a new business, management can be hands-on. In a growing business, management will need to be delegated. This will involve a clear idea of the direction of the business and of the integration of different tasks. It is, however, very important that the owner of the business has complete financial control.

Management of people and systems in a business

If it is necessary to employ staff in your business, then it is very important indeed that you have staff management strategies in place. When considering management planning in this area there are several considerations:

- What do you want from your staff-what is their function?
- How do you want them to perform-to achieve the task in hand?
- When do you want them to perform?
- What will be the salary structure and overall cost?

- What training will be provided to enable them to perform and to achieve greater job satisfaction?

The question of staff management and motivation, and the meshing of all the tasks to produce satisfactory outcomes is one of the most difficult areas of business management, alongside financial management.

Business control systems

Integral to all businesses is the need for a management information system. This will enable you to control your business effectively. The main areas where you will need an information system are:

- Financial performance-the ability to analyse how the company is doing and where it is going in the future
- An ongoing analysis of the marketplace
- A sales and distribution analysis
- A Physical resource analysis
- Human resource analysis.

The above is not exhaustive but are the key indicators from which you can draw information to enable you to manage the business in the present and the future. We will look at management systems later in the book.

Strategic threats

In business, there are ever present threats to the viability of your business and to your market share. These can be from new entrants into the marketplace, i.e., new companies, the threat of other products (substitute products). This could be an imitation of your product but a cheaper version, also the power of suppliers and buyers, effectively the ability to create monopolies and control prices and competitive rivalry from other companies.

All of these factors need to be analysed on a regular basis because if they aren't then you will find yourself at a sudden disadvantage.

Now read the key points from Chapter 3 overleaf

****

Key points from Chapter 3

- It is essential to have a crystal-clear idea of what the main objectives are for your business, both short and long-term

- Many business use the SMART criteria within which to set objectives

- Clear mission statements are essential for most businesses

- Businesses also carry out strategic analysis using PESTE analysis techniques

- It is necessary to carry out an audit of resources of your business to give you an idea of what will be needed in the future.

****

Chapter 4

Choosing The Structure of Your Business

There are various structures within which your business, whether traditional or online, can operate, and it is essential, when formulating your business plan that you understand the nature of each structure.

The sole or proprietary business
This is a business owned by one person. If you are operating alone then this may be suitable for your purposes. The person and the business are legally one and the same. It does not matter what or how you trade, as the business is inseparable from yourself, as opposed to a limited company, which is a separate entity. All financial risk is taken by that one person and all that person's assets are included in that risk. The one big advantage is that all decisions can be taken by the one person without interference.

A second advantage is that the administrative costs of running a sole business are small. If your business is VAT registered then you will need to keep records, as you will for Her Majesty's Revenue and Customs. However, there are no other legal requirements.

Partnerships
A partnership is a business where two or more people are joined by an agreement to run that business together. The agreement

is usually written, given the potential pitfalls that can arise. Liabilities which may arise are shared jointly and severally and this should be made clear to anyone entering a partnership. Even if you only have 1% of the business you will still be responsible for 100% of the liability. All personal assets of each partner are at risk if the business fails.

Decisions are taken jointly, as laid down by the partnership agreement. If the agreement lays down that the partners have differing decision making capacity dependent upon their shareholding, then it could be that, in a three-way partnership, the decision-making process may be hampered because a decision cannot be reached unless the major investor is present.

It is very important indeed to consider the nature of the agreement that you are entering, and it may also be advisable to take legal advice. Partnership usually reflects the way that business was capitalised although other factors may be taken into consideration. For example, an expert in a particular field may join with an investor to create a 50/50 partnership.

The Limited liability company

This type of company has evolved over the years and provides a framework within which a business can operate effectively. A limited company is usually the best vehicle for business, in all but the smallest of businesses. It is certainly the only sensible answer if capital is being introduced by those who are not actively involved in running the business (shareholders).

Shareholders inject capital and receive a return (dividend) in proportion to the capital they invest. They are eligible to attend an annual general meeting to approve or otherwise the way the

Directors are running the business. Annual General Meetings also determine how much of the profit will be distributed to shareholders.

Voting is in accordance with the number of shares held and the meeting can replace all or any of the directors if a majority are dissatisfied with them. Shareholders can, if a majority request, call an Extraordinary General Meeting to question directors about performance, outside the Cycle of Annual General Meetings.

Control of the company is in the hands of directors who are appointed by the shareholders to run the company on their behalf.

The company is a legal entity and stands alone from the directors and shareholders, who have limited liability.

When a company is created it will have an "Authorised Shareholding" That specifies the limit of a shareholder's liability. If all shares have been issued, then shareholders are not liable for any more debts that the company may accrue.

Looking at Franchises

A franchise is a business relationship between the franchisor who has a tried and tested business concept and the franchisee who will purchase the right to operate this business. A Franchise will involve a capital investment and payment of ongoing royalties or management fees based on sales-turnover or as a mark up on goods supplied for resale by the franchisor.

Advantages of a franchise

The main advantage of buying a franchise is that you will be buying a tried and tested business idea. Although usually not cheaper than starting your own business you are cutting out all the steps to achieving brand recognition. There are lots of benefits to buying a franchise, the main ones being:

- You will be purchasing a business concept that has been tried and tested in the marketplace
- Lower risks in initial set-up
- Business premises will all comply with a blueprint, which satisfies all regulations
- Publicity and ongoing marketing will be supplied by the franchisor as will training and education in the business field
- Networking opportunities will be available with other franchisors
- You will be operating in a defined geographical area.

In addition to the above, gaining funding to start a franchise is a good deal easier (depending on the franchise) than a start up business. In some circumstances, the franchisor may be able to offer funding for the franchise start up.

The disadvantages

Like most things in life, there are down sides. Once a franchise is purchased, it can be difficult to dispose of it as there are often terms imposed as to resale. Disputes can arise as to the royalty or management fee and there is also the possibility that the franchisor may fail leaving you with a business that may not be viable in isolation.

Different types of franchise

There are franchising opportunities available for all sorts of businesses. To assess whether a business is suitable for franchise there are several factors that you need to consider:

- The main one-the original business concept must have been tried and tested and proven to be a success.
- The franchise must have a distinct brand image and tried and tested methods
- Operation of the franchise must be profitable and provide the franchisor with a limit

If you look in some popular papers, such as Daltons Weekly, you can see a whole proliferation of businesses that are for sale as so-called franchises. It is, or should be, immediately obvious, that such businesses are highly suspect. It is necessary to look at the characteristics of a business for sale to gauge whether it is suitable for franchise. These characteristics will include:

- Products that have a very short life span in the market
- Businesses with minimal profitability
- Business with repeat business based on loyalty to an individual rather than a product or service
- Businesses that are specific to one geographical area.

There are three types of franchise:

- *Job franchise*-where effectively you are purchasing a job for yourself. These franchises will be one-person businesses and will require you to invest up to £20,000. Examples range from carpet cleaning to vehicle repair.
- *Business franchise.* Somewhat more complex as these involve the purchase of a complete business with staff. These

types of franchise can cost up to £100,000. Such franchises will include fast food outlets and print shops.
- *Investment franchises*. These are at the top end and usually include hotels and restaurants and a substantial investment will be required, often up to £1 million.

Beware when entering a franchise. As mentioned, there are many 'scams' out there. It is highly advisable to go to one of the franchising conferences, held in the main cities, to gain a better idea of what the franchising world is all about.

Patents and Registered designs

To grow, industry must continually create and develop new ideas. Innovation is expensive and innovators need protection, to ensure that others cannot pirate their ideas. All the above items are known as "intellectual property" and, except for copyright, to register and protect your intellectual property, you need to contact the patent office. Their address can be obtained from the Chartered Institute of Patent Agents, whose number is at the rear of this book.

A Patent

If you or your company have produced what you consider is a unique product or process, it is very important to register it as soon as possible, before disclosing it to anyone. The granting of a patent gives the patentee a monopoly to make, use or sell an invention for a fixed period. This is currently a maximum of twenty years.

Registered designs

This involves registering what you consider to be a new design. The proprietor must register before offering for sale in the U.K the new design.

Trademarks

A trademark is a means of identification-whether a word or a logo- which is used during trade to identify and distinguish to the purchaser that the goods in question are yours. A good trademark is a very important marketing aid, and you are strongly advised to register it.

Service marks

This register extends the trademark to cover not only goods but services. If you are running a hotel for example, you can now register your service mark if you have one.

Copyright

Unlike the other four categories, copyright is established by evidence of creation, and protection is automatic. To safeguard your position, it might be sensible to deposit your work with your bank or your solicitor or send a copy of your work to yourself by registered post. It should be noted that there is no copyright attached to a name or title, only the work itself.

Having given thought to the likely structure of your business, and factors such as intellectual property we need now to consider, in chapter four, the right location for your business and questions relating to the employment and management of staff.

Key points from Chapter 4

- There are several structures within which your business can operate, and it is vital that you find the correct one for you.

- These structures apply to all types of business, whether traditional or online.

- You can operate as a sole trader, partnership, limited company, or franchise.

- You should consider areas of patent and copyright that may affect your business.

****

Ch. 5

Location/Premises/Employees-Making the Right Choices and Decisions

---

Location of your business

To be within easy reach of your customers may be vital or it may be totally unimportant. If you have a traditional retail business, location is a major consideration. If you are in mail order or operate an online business, you can operate from anywhere in the country so far as your customers are concerned, although there are many other considerations.

If you are a wholesaler, do you require a showroom? If you are operating a factory, do you anticipate the requirement for a factory shop? Is it simply a question of being conveniently located for your customers or are you relying on passing trade?

It is vital that, in assessing the right location, you first clearly define the extent to which you need to make yourself accessible to your customers.

In an ideal world, you should be looking to acquire the right accommodation for your scale of operation today and for your expansion plans this year, next year and some years in the future. This applies whether you are looking for a shop, an office, a workshop, or a factory unit. Before you start looking for new premises, work out carefully just what it is you need now.

The important questions to consider are:
- How much office/storage space/workshop/showroom do you need?
- How many square feet of employee's facilities?
- How much car parking space?
- How much outside storage for deliveries, storage, and packing?

If you are uncertain as to what precisely you need, or you feel that the shape of your business is going to alter substantially and in the short term, do not commit yourself to a hefty purchase, or even as much as a five-year lease. Go instead for a temporary solution, while you determine what your long-term requirements are likely to be.

Never enter a lengthy commitment unless you feel that the premises are likely to suit you in the long term. Whether you are buying a freehold or acquiring a lease, take independent professional advice on the value. Hire a surveyor who will tell you whether the asking price or rent is fair. Whatever your business, the cost of your premises is going to represent a major overhead. If you get it wrong, you will go out of business.

It is essential to establish that not only can the property be used for the purpose for which you want it, but also that the planning consent will cover any future business development.

Working from home
Particularly if you are starting a new business, maybe an online business, the idea of working from home is attractive. It enables you to keep your overheads to a minimum, allows you to work the

long hours necessary in the establishment of a business, and leaves your options open, if the business does not work out, you are not committed to an industrial property. It needs to be recognized, however, that working from home can cause considerable problems.

Strictly speaking, if you plan to run a business from home, almost certainly you will need approval or permission either from someone or some authority. There are two kinds of restrictions which may affect your ability to run your business from home. The first is a series of contractual relationships which you may have already entered, such as a tenancy or lease. The second is that imposed by local authorities-planning, highways, health, and safety.

However, if your business is internet based and you are carrying no stock then you may not be affected by these restrictions.

Planning permission

If you want to make a significant alteration to your house to accommodate your business, you will need planning permission or building regulations approval. This includes building an extension, loft conversion, in fact almost anything except extremely simple alterations

Change of use

Local authorities state that consent must be sought for any change of use. The interpretation of change of use is difficult but what you must decide is whether what you wish to do constitutes a genuine material change of use of the building. You should make sure that you have insurance to cover your business activity within your home. If you have an accident which occurs as a direct result of your business, then your insurance will not cover it.

Health and Safety at work

Whatever your position in relationship to your premises, i.e., leasehold, or freehold, under the terms of the Health and Safety at Work Act 1974, you have certain obligations to protect yourself, your staff, your customers, and your suppliers. Health and Safety Legislation is very important, and attention should be paid to it.

Inspectors

There are two types of inspector-local authority inspectors and fire authority inspectors. Local Authority inspectors are concerned with premises where the main activities are:

- The sale or storage of goods for retail or wholesale distribution.
- Office activities
- Catering Services
- Provision of residential accommodation
- Consumer services provided in shop premises
- Dry Cleaning in coin operated units in launderettes
- The keeping of wild animals for exhibition to the public
- Fire Authority inspectors

The fire authority requires that a place of work should have a fire certificate, and for your business to get a fire certificate, the premises need to be inspected. The fire authority will wish to see that there is adequate provision for a means of escape in case of fire, and the necessary amount of equipment. The Fire inspectors will advise you whether these facilities are inadequate, tell you how they can be put right and then re-inspect the premises when you have carried out the necessary work.

Employing People

At first you may be able to run your business by yourself or with help from your family. But if not, as your business expands, you may need to employ people. Before doing this, some businesses may consider it worthwhile subcontracting work. This may be more cost effective in ironing out short-term trading highs and lows. However, if you do need to take on employees, then you must do certain things.

What are my responsibilities as an employer?

You must give every employee a written statement of terms of employment. At the time of publication, by law, all employees working 16 or more hours a week must be given a written statement of terms after they have worked 13 weeks in the job. This statement must include the following:

- name of employer
- name of employee, job title and description
- hours of work
- pay details, including how often the employee is paid
- holidays
- grievance procedures

- sickness and injury procedures
- pension schemes
- length of notice needed to end employment
- disciplinary rules, including dress and behaviour

National Insurance Contributions

If you employ anybody, either full time or part time, you must take tax and national insurance contributions (NIC's) from their wages, and you must also pay the employers share of the NIC's, always consult your local contributions agency office. There are different tax and National Insurance Rules depending on your circumstances.

Discrimination and the law

It is against the law for an employer or a would-be employer to advertise a job that in anyway discriminates against race or sex. After taking on an employee, the anti-discrimination laws still apply to all other parts of the employees' job, including wages and holidays.

Trade Unions

Make sure that you know about the various laws which safeguard your employees' rights to choose whether to join a trade union.

Tax and National Insurance-more details

Once you regularly employ people, you are responsible for deducting their income tax and National Insurance Contributions, and paying your own employers NI contributions.

When you take on someone, you need to tell your local tax

office. You will be sent documents which will show you how much you need to take out of each employee's wages, and where to send the money. You must record each employees' earnings and tax and National Insurance Contributions, and tell your local tax office about these amounts each year.

In the case of National Insurance, the contributions for your employees will be in two parts. You must pay one part and your employee will pay the other. These contributions depend on how much you pay your employee. HMRC will collect them at the same time as they collect any tax. For more advice on National Insurance go to:

www.gov.uk/government/organisations/hm-revenue-customs. This is the Gov.uk site dealing with NI enquiries.

Your personal insurance depends on your circumstances. If you are a company director, you will be treated in a similar way to your employees. You will be classed as an employee of your company and will pay contributions in the same way as your employees. But there is no special way to assess directors National Insurance.

You should contact the Contributions Agency Office for advice on this matter. If you are a sole trader, or partner, your contributions will be charged at the same rate each week. You must pay them every month by direct debit or every three months when you receive a bill. You may also have to pay an extra contribution for any profits your company makes. This is assessed and collected along with Income tax.

You should tell the contribution's agency office as soon as you become self-employed.

The law and you as an employer

Having considered some of the main issues involved in employing people, you may want to become more acquainted with the following issues and how the law deals with them:

- terms of employment
- redundancy
- insolvency
- pregnancy
- suspension on medical grounds
- sick leave
- health and safety
- union membership
- itemised pay statements
- continuous employment
- time off for public duties
- unfair dismissal
- rights on ending employment
- union secret ballots
- limit on payment
- race discrimination
- sex discrimination
- equal pay
- disabled workers
- picketing
- Pensions (Automatic Enrolment of Employees)

Location/Premises/Employees-Making the Right Choices and Decisions

Although all the above areas may not affect you, particularly in the early stages of development, if you do intend to employ staff then you should at least acquaint yourself with the areas.

Recruiting and motivating employees-doing it yourself

You can do your own recruiting by advertising locally or in appropriate papers. Or you could write to colleges and schools for candidates.

Job centres and employment agencies

The Job Centre, the Job Club, or the local careers office are all in business to fit people to jobs. Job Centres or careers offices give their services for free, but an employment agency could cost you as much as 20% of the employees first year's salary.

Training

Training is necessary to make sure that staff know why and how a job must be done. It can also help make them more efficient and help increase their productivity. Investing wisely in staff training pays off in the long run.

The personal approach

The better you treat your employees, the better they will treat you. If you are well mannered, punctual, and committed they will be too. Show them that they are valued, encourage their interest in the business and ask them for suggestions. They will probably respond positively but don't be patronising. Have confidence in your workforce and allow them to get on with the job. Checking everything they do creates resentment and not much else. All good managers can delegate. Good delegation is what management is all about. You could also set targets and give bonuses. This way, you will encourage your employees to work harder. As a result, you will increase productivity and waste less time. Payment-you must always pay wages on time and at competitive rates, considering the minimum wage and the affordable wage. Show appreciation-praise for a job well done is a real incentive. But try not to be over friendly. This is difficult when you are working one to one, but it might reduce your authority and it will be difficult to take a firm line if you ever need to.

Now read the key points from Chapter 5

****

Key points from Chapter 5

- The location of your business may be important depending on the nature of the business.

- When considering premises size and space are key considerations, as is car parking.

- Depending on your business, it may be possible to work from home.

- When employing people, you will need to be familiar with employment law and also the structure of the various government agencies that exist to help the would-be employer.

****

SECTION 3

MARKETING AND PRICING STRATEGIES

- Working Out Your Marketing Strategy

- Working Out Prices of Your Product

Ch. 6

Marketing Your Business

The next step in formulating your business plan is to look at sales, which in turn means looking at the market and considering the most appropriate form of market research. Sales are vital to any business. Whatever you produce, and whichever business you are operating, whether traditional or online, or both, you must be able to sell your product. This is necessary to survive.

You must be satisfied that there is a demand for your proposed business, and you must be able to determine how you can investigate the market in which you want to operate and how many potential clients there are in either the catchment area you operate in or the wider area. If you work in publishing for example, then clearly the market for your product would be different for that of a baker or butcher or plumber. A lot of thought needs to be given to this area.

Market Research

The tool that is used to determine demand for a product is market research. Market research can be cheap and simple or highly complex depending on how you approach it and what you might want to find out.

Market research, or effective market research should be able to provide you with information as to what people want and how much they want and what they will pay for it. Competition that might exist should also come to light. You should not be put off by competition nor should you believe that because there appears to be no local supplier that what you produce will sell. No supplier may mean no demand and competition may mean established demand.

The concept behind all market research is simple, however the practice is often not and unless you have a lot of money the costs may be prohibitive. A good example might be a supermarket. A potential supermarket would want to know concrete facts to establish demand. For example, in terms of the percentage of the population, the average number of visits made to a supermarket each year. This they may well be able to establish from their own records if they are part of a chain.

Secondly, they would want to know what distance people are prepared to travel to visit a supermarket. This will vary a lot but they would be interested in establishing a national average.

With these two facts the supermarket can then establish the catchment area population for the proposed supermarket. Now they need to know something about the competition. How many supermarkets are there in the catchment zone which might influence the proposed supermarket? This is easily established. However, more difficult to determine is the effect on your potential business. If we suppose that the supermarket decides that only 30% of the catchment area is exposed to competition and that they expect that 50% of that 30% would continue to use the supermarkets, they presently use. This means an adjustment to predicted customer base.

However, competition comes from other shops not just supermarkets This is why calculations are based on average figures since this additional competition will be standard throughout the country. A survey will be carried out in the locality to check that there are no special factors to consider- special factors which may cause adjustments to the predicted customer base either way.

The next question to be considered is what is the average spend per visit per customer? Supermarkets will almost certainly be able to answer that one from existing records. From this data, they can predict gross sales and the net operating profit. If this is not high enough to justify the expenditure, they might be reluctant to proceed with building a supermarket.

The above is a simple model and does not consider several complications, but it does give an idea of how market research is carried out. There are two very important factors to be considered-average conditions in the industry and catchment area population, or a knowledge of that population. Although the example given covers selling to the public the same principle applies when considering selling to other business.

It may be possible to determine industry averages by approaching trade associations. A visit to the bank is also very worthwhile as most high street banks keep statistics which they would be willing to make available. A further source of statistics might be a major supplier in an industry.

Somewhat easier to determine is the magnitude of the target market. Businesses generally fall into one or two categories: those where the customer comes to the business to place the order and those where the business goes to the customer to get the order.

In the first category, the size of your target market will be a percentage of the local population. The size of the population can be found by contacting the records office at your local authority. The percentage which applies to your proposed business will be far harder to determine. The classic method is simple, ask a large enough sample to provide an accurate picture. This is easier said than done. A great deal of research experience is necessary to be able to design a questionnaire which can elicit all the right information.

If you can afford it, you could consider employing a market research agency to assist you. If you cannot afford it then you should spend time considering exactly what you want to ask and what you are trying to establish. There are many other places which will hold the sort of information you might need. Your local training enterprise agency (TEC) or the trade association relevant to your business will be only too pleased to assist you.

Once you have established your target market, you might wish to consider exactly how you sell to that market. Easy if you have a shop in the middle of a busy shopping area, or a web-based business, easier than if you produce books and must cast your net far wider. It might be useful at this stage to look at marketing in a little more depth.

Marketing generally

You have carried out some form of research and now you are in a position where you wish to bring to people's attention your product. Obviously different media are more suited to some businesses than others. Marketing covers a whole range of activities designed to "identify, anticipate, and satisfy customer needs at a profit" (Chartered Institute of Marketing). Three questions need to be looked at:

- When do customers want needs satisfied?
- How do the customers want the need fulfilled?
- How much are the customers prepared to pay for that fulfilment?

Having found the answers to those questions we have to decide how best to communicate to the target market our ability to meet their needs at a price that they can afford-and communicate that ability to them at a price that we can afford. There are various options that we can consider. However, some of these options are expensive and may well not be within your reach.

Advertising

Advertising takes various forms. It is exceedingly difficult, unless you have deep pockets, to try to deduce the real effectiveness of whichever form of advertising you decide to employ. For example, is it cost effective to spend £800 on a small advert in a tabloid for one day if that £800 could be spent on something longer lasting?

Advertising hoardings and posters are one way. These tend to cover not only billboards but also tubes trains and buses. Hoardings are seen repeatedly by a wide and ever-changing audience in the locality of your choice. They are usually inexpensive.

Leaflets

Leaflets can be distributed on a door-to-door basis (either to other businesses or to individual residences) or they can be given to individuals in the street. However, leaflets can also be thrown away as many see them as junk mail. The result is that leaflets tend to have a low strike rate. Leaflets can also be delivered as inserts in magazines and newspapers. Magazines direct leaflets to specific audiences and newspapers to local areas. Both can prove expensive and again will be discarded often.

A more effective use of leaflets is to have them available in places where the target market will see them. The classic case here is for businesses offering non-residential facilities for holidaymakers. These can usually be found in hotels and guesthouses. Another use of the leaflet is that of a poster in a newsagent or on other notice boards. This can be effective when being used to attract a defined group of the population who gather in one place where leaflets cannot be made available. Universities or schools might be a good example.

Directories

Directories will fall into two categories-local and trade. Local directories such as yellow pages are well known mediums of advertising, and they are reasonably priced, sometimes free. However, the effectiveness of such advertising depends on what you are doing and where the ad is placed. Some businesses tend towards directories such as Thompson's because they have less advertisers and are cheaper.

Trade directories are different by their nature. They are unlikely to benefit new businesses as they can be expensive and are in some cases, nationally distributed. This is of little use if your business is local, of more use if your product is distributed nationally. There are now several local area and regional directories, often produced by trade associations. Some are available as a book or on disc for use with computers.

Those who subscribe to the disc system often receive monthly or quarterly updates.

Advertising in magazines

Magazines fall into three categories-general national, local or specialist. Magazines tend to be more expensive to advertise in than newspapers but can be more effective. Magazines have a longer life expectancy than newspapers and are often passed on to other readers. Specialist magazines are read by specific people who may form part of your desired target audiences. It is worthwhile bearing in mind that most magazines are national.

Newspaper advertising

National newspapers can obviously reach a lot of people but also tend to be expensive. They are also of little value to those offering local services. Local newspaper advertising can be more effective and cheaper. Free newspapers are cheaper but can be less effective as they also tend to be seen as junk mail.

Television advertising

It is highly unlikely that television advertising will be relevant in the early years of a business. To launch a television advertising campaign is very expensive indeed. Therefore, this medium will only be a consideration later, if at all.

Radio advertising

This form of advertising would only be effective If there are enough listeners in the target market. However, in the right circumstances it can be useful and relatively inexpensive. Timing is very important in this medium as you need to target your slots at the most appropriate times and on the most appropriate programme for your intended target audience.

Using an advertising agent

Whether or not an advertising agency is employed will be a matter for the individual business concerned. This decision is down to cost. All businesses placing advertising should set an advertising budget. It could be that placing part of your budget with an agent proves far more cost effective than designing your own campaign.

Agents are usually good at designing and placing adverts and can negotiate discounts with various media. It is certainly worthwhile consulting an agent to get an idea of what they can do for you, at the same time raising your own awareness of the direction you should be taking.

Direct mail

Direct mail falls into two categories: untargeted or blanket mailing or targeted. Targeted mail is usually far more effective as untargeted mail can be very expensive and wasteful. Existing customers of a business are well defined and easily targeted. The secret with direct mail is to keep it short, simple and do it as often as is necessary.

Using sales representatives or agents

Whether or not you choose to use representatives or agents will depend on several factors. Where there are few sales required and the selling of a good is complex there may be the need for a representative. Where the product is simple and can be described in an advertisement or leaflet it is unlikely to be necessary to use a representative. There are two main types of representation, the representative or agent.

The representative is a paid member of staff who may or may not receive a bonus or commission based on results. All the representatives running costs will be borne by the business. An agent is a freelance who meets his or her own costs and is paid only on results.

The advantage of using the representative is that he or she uses their entire time devoted to your business and is under your total control. The agent costs little to run. However, he or she is not totally dedicated to your business. If other products are easier to sell, he may ignore yours altogether.

As you can see, there are several ways to reach your target audience once that target audience has been defined. A lot of thought needs to be given to market research and marketing. All too often, they are the first areas to go through the window in search of savings or simply because you are too busy. However, well-defined marketing can produce a corresponding increase in profits and a clear strategy is an essential part of any business plan.

Online marketing

Having looked at more traditional ways of advertising a business, all of which are relevant, it is now time to look at the process of Internet marketing. This is relevant whether you are a traditional or web-based business.

Each business has its own overall budget and goals and targets. In the ideal world it would be nice to be able to invest in both offline and online marketing. However, the reality for most businesses, particularly start-ups, is that funds are limited. In this case, it is crucial to understand the techniques used in online marketing. (We will be discussing additional factors relating to web-based businesses in more depth in chapter 8)

Search engine optimization

Most users of the internet will begin the buying process with a search engine. Search engines are enormously powerful and therefore it is essential that your website is built, maintained, and updated to be both customer and search engine friendly. Effective search engine optimization is about making your website visible to the search engines, primarily Google.

Making your site visible to search engines

Your site must be seen to be ranked. Google uses software called Googlebot to scan individual web pages on the internet and what it finds has a direct impact on how thoroughly your site is indexed and how it can rank in the natural Search Engine Results Pages (SERPS).

Quality content

Good content is the key to a good website. Good content will sell your product. Good content will mean that more and more users will visit your site and become consumers of your products and services. In addition, if you have good content then other websites will want to link up to your site therefore increasing the flow of traffic. If your site and its content is seen as good by Google, then it will be ranked higher. People looking for a specific good or service will go straight to your site, bypassing the competition. However, to ensure that this is the case, your site should be well designed and regularly maintained and updated.

A by-product of creating good content on your website is that other websites will want to link to your content. This can only be good because it puts your website in a position of being an authority on your given product or service. It will result in more traffic to your site and will attract the attention of Google, improving your rankings. It is no good developing a site which looks attractive and then not maintaining it or trying to optimize your rankings. This will set you back and if you are relying more on people finding your site, as opposed to the more traditional forms of marketing, then it is essential to have an ongoing plan for updating and promoting your site.

The use of key words and phrases
You will want to find your main, or niche, keywords and concentrate on writing content to exploit the words. Keywords are the tool through which those who search the web find your unique product. If you are selling bathrooms for example you will want to come up with as many associated words as possible such as 'designer bathrooms' or 'Victorian bathrooms' in other words, try to differentiate and provide as many entries as possible for the user. To just use the word 'bathroom' will severely limit the access to your own site.

Search engine marketing
SEM, Paid Search or PPC advertising is a broad subject that will

require research on your part to ensure that you know what you are doing before you invest heavily. SEM allows you to display an advert on the Search Engine Results Pages or the Search Engines network of publisher websites which you can target to display only to users searching for specific keywords or phrases related to your business. You control your account totally, from the text or images of the advert to how much you wish to spend.

If you elect to run PPC adverts with Google, then your ads will be displayed above and to the right of the organic or natural search results, i.e. the sponsored area. Google calls its program Adwords, which is where the search engine makes most of its profits. There are several reasons why search engine marketing is effective:

- It is quick to get started
- You are in control of what you spend
- Your campaigns give you instant visibility

What Google has done with Adwords is to create an online auction for every keyword and phrase in every language. The more competitive a keyword, the higher the price. This is how Google makes its money. You should start your Adwords campaign with a small budget, dip your toe in the water, to see how you go. Setting up an account is simple enough and you should ensure that you read the help and FAQs on the site before committing yourself.

Adwords works by charging you a fee every time someone clicks on your advert-the more you are willing to pay in comparison to others bidding for the same keywords and the better your landing page is (Quality Score) the higher up the sponsored links you will be placed. The bigger your budget, the more users will be shown your advert and the more that will click through. As soon as your budget has been spent, your advert is taken off until the next day. This allows you to keep tight control of your marketing spend and allows you to see very quickly if the campaign is working and to measure the return on your investment.

Purchasing traffic
When you enter Google Adwords or place a banner ad on another website you are in effect buying traffic to your site. There are some unscrupulous companies around that charge you for delivering visitors to your site and then don't deliver.

Legitimate performance marketing companies do exist, and they are aware of the business need for traffic. They are also quite sophisticated and can direct the right sort of traffic to your site. Performance marketing companies invest heavily in building up their own network of users or publisher's websites which they then exploit by showing their advertiser's (your) sales message to their network. By carefully categorizing and segmenting their user base, they can effectively ensure that your pages are shown to relevant users. If someone wants law books for example, they will only show your advertisement to those interested in law books.

Depending on the size and nature of the performance marketing company you can specify the countries in which you want your advert to be shown or even the approximate age or gender of the target audience. The more specific your requirements the more you will be charged for the service. However, because it is performance based, you will only pay when the campaign results in a conversion. The following are several companies that offer Performance marketing:

Burst www.burstmedia.com
ValueClick Media www.conversantmedia.com

There are many more!

Email marketing

Email marketing is an effective way to send your message before you have had a chance of building up your own database of customers. Performance marketing companies will provide lists that are segmented by interest. You will need to check with the provider that all addresses have been cleared and have given their consent to receive third party promotional emails. I receive many such emails every day which I have not consented to and which I delete, so it is important to do your homework beforehand.

Affiliation (as advertiser)

There are a wide variety of affiliation networks available which marry advertisers to publishers. Most networks charge new advertisers a set-up fee which gives your business access to the network of affiliates. Set-up fees can be hefty, so you need to go into this with care. In addition, most networks charge advertisers a monthly fee which covers continued access to the network. Ongoing performance can be monitored through the networks portal and affiliates reports can be generated. The strongest aspect of affiliation is payment on performance. You only pay a commission if your affiliate delivers a lead, registration, or sale. You are free to pay as much or as little as you want for each of these conversions. Affiliates take campaigns seriously and invest time, money, and effort to promote advertiser's products and services. The relationship is two way, and you also must be serious, keeping them up to date with new products, pricing and any offers or promotions that you intend to run. As with all aspects of business, good communication is the key.

Using vouchers and coupons

The use of vouchers and coupons to promote and sell products, usually at a discount, is becoming increasingly popular with online business. The idea has been around forever, being used for all sorts of off-line business but it is now being used for online trading. Coupons usually allow customers, whether existing or new, to benefit from a promotion by entering a code online at the point of purchasing. The utilization of the code will modify the customers order in some way corresponding to the offer. These coupons can be printed and distributed through print media, handed out in the street as a flyer or as part of promotional literature, or through any other medium. They can also be distributed online by adding the coupon to a social media post such as Facebook or Twitter. They can also be sent to existing customers in a mailshot. The use of coupons as part of your selling strategy will require some work to your site and again this is what you will be asking your web designer to do for you.

Co-registration

Co-registration is a lead and customer acquisition strategy used by numerous brands. It is performance based-you only pay on results. Co-registration involves placing a short text or image advertisement for your company on the registration pages of high-volume third-party websites or landing pages. Usually, you are sharing the page with other advertisers who sell similar products or services, or the page is themed in such a way as to link the advertisers. This method of promotion allows users to request additional information about your product or service and in turn provides you with their contact details.

Co-registration allows you to build a permission based, targeted database of consumers interested in your service and, depending on the volume of the third-party site, allows you to develop lists very quickly.

Rich media

Rich media is, basically, videos, pod casts and other images that will serve to improve your visibility and differentiate you from other sites selling similar products. Most shop windows have excellent displays and lure customers in. Web portals should be the same and a short video can do wonders when it comes to displaying your product or telling customers more about you and your company and what products or services you sell.

Social media

Social media, such as Facebook and Twitter is now so widespread that it would be foolish not to advertise your existence on their sites. By opening accounts with platforms such as Facebook, Twitter and Linked In you will be able to reach your potential audience and hear what is being said about your company, product, or service.

Blogging

Adding a blog to your business website is a simple procedure for any web developer and the quality and customization options from the big players such as Wordspace and Blogger leaves very little need to develop your own platform. A blog will allow you to produce articles, presenting news and comment about your business and its operations. Blogging helps to develop brand building and may provide you with competitive advantage.

Market places

Market places such as Ebay can be very useful. Although initially conceived as a site where individuals can buy and sell, it now has a facility for professional sellers. Ebay and Amazon in the UK, and Priceminister and Play in Europe, among a few others, provide online business the opportunity to enjoy a worldwide audience by listing your products or services and offering them to their enormous customer base. By paying a listing fee, or a monthly fee plus a share or percentage of the sale price, your business can gain enormous reach within a very short time.

To make it easy for businesses to sell via marketplace sites, these online sellers offer a route to professional sellers to be able to bulk load their products. This is achieved through XML, CSV or through an online portal. There will be some work involved on your side adapting your product database to the platforms particular product classification rules, but once that is done, it is usually a straightforward process loading your products. The listing fee, commission on sale and other fees can tend to be high if you are selling low margin items. However, the sheer size of the audience can make it worthwhile. As with many other things, it is a case of trying it, dipping your toe in the water and see whether it is worth carrying on.

Now read the key points from Chapter 6 overleaf.

****

Key Points from Chapter 6

- It is vital that you understand the market and the demand for your product.

- Effective market research, and an understanding of how this works, is vital to your business.

- Marketing covers a whole range of activities designed to identify, anticipate, and satisfy customers at a profit.

- There are several ways of reaching customers to determine demand, advertising, leaflets, television, radio, direct mail and more. You may consider using an agent to help you.

****

Ch. 7

Pricing Your Product-Creating A Pricing Plan

A well thought out pricing plan is essential to the future prosperity of your business and will also help you to make the most of your opportunities.

To develop the right pricing plan for your business, you need to start by working out what your costs are. You need to look at what your competitors are charging and try to estimate what your service or product is worth to your customers. By knowing what costs, you are incurring, you will be able to work out what your "break-even" point is. How much do you need to sell before your business covers all its costs, including your own (essential) drawings, but before it makes a profit? Unless you can identify what, your break-even point is, you could operate at a loss, without realising until it is too late.

Your costs

Costs can be divided into fixed (overheads) and variable (direct) costs. Fixed costs include your essential personal expenses, such as Mortgage, food etc, as well as rent, heating and lighting, wages, and interest charges. They tend to stay the same no matter how much you sell. Variable costs, however, increase or decrease according to your level of sales. The most obvious cost here is the actual cost of materials required to manufacture the product but can include other things such as transport, postage, or additional labour. The price you charge for your product must cover all the variable costs and contribute towards your overheads.

Outlined below is an example of a break-even point.

Fred Peters Car Wash Ltd	Cost per Annum
Personal Drawings	10,000
National Insurance	294
Tax	500
Stationary	100
Advertising	400
Telephone	320
Depreciation of Van (over 5 years)	1,000
Petrol	900
Servicing	300
Road Tax Fund	130
Insurance	320
Business Insurance	140
Materials	200
Depreciation of Equipment	200
Bank Loan £3,000 @ 12%	200
Bank Charges	100
Accountants Fees	300
TOTAL	£15,404

Fred's essential personal drawings to cover his family expenses is £10,000. He operates a small car wash. He expects to work for 46 weeks a year, allowing for holidays, sickness etc. He estimates that he will work 38 hours per week.

His annual output is therefore:

46 weeks a year Times 38 hours times 0.5 cars per hour = 874

His break-even point is:
15,404
―――――
874

= £17.62 per car

After researching the market in his area, Fred believes he can confidently charge £20 per car, which will give him a reasonable profit.

Competitors Prices
Unless your service or product is much better than others on the market, you would be unwise to charge a price which is too far above your competitors, as you will find sales very hard to achieve. On the other hand, a low price often implies low quality or low standards.

Competing on price alone is a poor option. It is especially important for small businesses to differentiate themselves by other means, such as personal service, convenience, or special skills. Customers rarely buy on price alone and it is worth remembering that you can more easily reduce your prices than put them up. If, when you work out what your prices should be, they do not cover your costs-look again at how you might make your business viable. For example, could you reduce any of your variable costs, could you get supplies more cheaply, can you negotiate a discount or find an alternative supplier? On your fixed costs, could you trim any other expenditure?

Think again about what you are offering. Could it be improved and sold at a higher price? Can you sell different products for more money to increase your profits? Would sales increase if you put up your prices and spent the extra income on advertising and promotion? Every cost incurred in running your business must be recovered either by what you charge for your time, or by the amount you charge for your products. Profits will be made only after all your costs have been covered. But you may decide to use different prices in different situations. For example, a plumber offering a 24-hour service might decide to charge a premium rate for his services if he is called out during the night to deal with an emergency, a different rate for weekends and another rate for normal working hours.

Achieving a range of prices for the variety of skills offered, considering the time you would be likely to spend on each job can give you the flexibility to stay competitive, yet still provide a satisfactory income.

Now read the key points from chapter 7

****

Key points from Chapter 7

- A well thought out pricing plan is vital to your business.

- Always consider hidden costs when pricing goods.

- Unless your service or product is much better than others on the market, you would be unwise to charge a price which is too far above your competitors, as you will find sales very hard to achieve. On the other hand, a low price often implies low quality or low standards.

****

SECTION 4

FINANCIAL CONTROL

- **RAISING FINANCE FOR YOUR START UP**

- **SYSTEMS FOR FINANCIAL CONTROL**

Ch.8

Raising Finance for Your Business

Raising finance for your business can be difficult or relatively easy depending on the viability of your business and its ability to meet repayments and the nature and type of assets that your business owns. It is true to say that raising finance is harder and more expensive than it has been for a very long time. However, you should consider the options below. There are several alternatives when it comes to raising finance:

Investment of own funds
At the outset it is almost certain that you will have to invest some of your own time and money into your business. The investment will be financial, i.e., money which is an injection of your own funds into the business. If you are trading as a limited company this could take the form of a loan to the company or share capital. If you intend to operate as a sole trader or a partnership this will be owner's or partners capital.

The non-financial investment will take the form of assets that you already own, such as tools and equipment, or a vehicle. These will need to be valued for inclusion into the firms records and an accountant will almost certainly need to be employed to ensure that they are correctly valued and comply with relevant guidelines.

Short-term finance

This type of finance is usually referred to as working capital finance. It is used to finance working capital and pay creditors and is then itself repaid following receipts of funds from debtors. The most common type of short-term finance is provided by banks in the form of an overdraft.

Trade credit

Obtaining credit from suppliers is also a type of short-term finance. The terms of credit with a supplier will vary according to the type of your business and the supplier.

Factoring

Factoring services have been used increasingly by small businesses in the last ten years or so, particularly those businesses providing services to large companies or corporations which tend not to pay invoices for up to six months. Factoring enables you to bridge the gap between sending out an invoice and receiving payment. Factoring invoices has the advantage that you can receive immediate payment against an invoice, usually around 80% of face value. It has the disadvantage that there is a cost attached to it and it also has a stigma attached to it and can unsettle those with whom you do business as it is perceived that you have cashflow problems.

Invoice discounting

This operates on broadly the same principle as factoring but with several differences:

- Control of the sales ledger is retained by you, and it will be your responsibility to chase bad debtors, unlike factoring where the bank concerned (usually a bank) will undertake this function
- Because control is retained by you the existence of the arrangement won't be evident to customers

Long-term finance

If the finance is to be used to purchase any fixed asset, then you must obtain long-term finance. It is good practice to raise the finance based on the life cycle of that fixed asset.

Business loans

Business loans can be raised from several sources. The usual source will be your bank if you already have a business account. Some loans are secured, and some are unsecured. With all forms of business loans, you need to know exactly what the terms are. Most loans are from £1,000-£1million and are repaid from 1 year to 20 years. You should consider the merits and demerits of fixed rate loans and variable loans. This will be influenced by the economic climate currently prevailing.

Hire purchase and leasing

Hire purchase is a very flexible and relatively easy to obtain type of funding, often used to purchase assets. Leasing is a flexible form of funding. A lease is negotiated with the lessor. Assets that are leased can vary from office furniture to heavy machinery to vehicles. Leasing is distinguished from hiring. Hiring requires the hirer to select an item which is already in stock whilst with leasing an item can be chosen from any manufacturer or supplier. The subsequent lease agreement will be tailor made for the asset involved.

There are three types of leases:
- Finance lease
- Operating lease
- Contract hire

Finance leases
With a finance lease, the lessor pays for the asset and becomes the owner. The lessee then pays a hire charge that covers the capital cost of the asset and interest and service charges. The lessee is responsible for all subsequent maintenance and insurance.

Operating lease
This type of lease is, in the main, undertaken by the manufacturer of products that tend to be highly specialised or technical. The lease will usually provide that the lessor is responsible for all future servicing, maintenance and updating of equipment.

Contract hire
This is like an operating lease. One of the most common uses of contract hire is to finance a fleet of motor vehicles. In the case of contract hire, the lessor will take responsibility for all future maintenance and costs, the lessee has only to find fuel costs.

Soft loans

These sorts of loans are available usually on more generous terms and are made through local Enterprise Agencies and are available when conventional funding is not. There are other forms of finance available which would not really be relevant to small business startups, such as equity finance, where a proportion of the business is given up for finance, and venture capital, which is only really for larger investments. It is highly advisable, if you need more detailed advice or assistance concerning finance, that you contact your local business advice centre.

These centres are there to assist all potential or existing businesses and will provide someone who is expert in this field to advise you.

Grants

If you are looking to secure a small amount of money, a grant or combination of grants may be more suitable for your business. This is one of the cheapest forms of finance but be aware of the non-financial conditions that may be attached to the grant. These could be the number and types of people employed and restrictions on what the money can be spent on. Grants range from local initiatives run by local development agencies to Business Link funding as well as private funds across the country.

Grants and where to get them

There are many thousands of sources of grants, and it is not possible to cover them all here. They can, however, be grouped into several categories.

National government

Grants for small firms come from both the UK government but also the Scottish Parliament, Welsh, and Northern Ireland Assemblies. Each of these has its own departments and agencies, which hand out the money based on its own criteria and objectives. There are over one hundred of these bodies but among the most important are:

- Department for Business, Energy, and Industrial Strategy
- Department for Employment and Learning
- Department for Environment, Food and Rural Affairs
- Scottish Executive
- Welsh Government
- Enterprise Ireland

Local

In addition to the many local government authorities, there are several locally based agencies and organisations which have been established specifically to support and encourage enterprise at a local level. One such example is www.gov.uk which has a grants and support directory where you can search grant schemes by sector or location.

Eligibility for grants

Each grant scheme has its own set of criteria to determine whether a firm or project is worthy of its money. There is no business or industry sector that is excluded from applying for funds. Most schemes apply without major restrictions but on those that do eligibility tends to fall into three main categories: location; size and industry.

As you can see there are a plethora of grants. A good starting point to research grant giving bodies is the Enterprise Advisory Service www.arcweb.com.

Crowdfunding and Peer-to-Peer Loans

Crowdfunding and peer-to-peer lending have been through turbulent times and the Financial Conduct Authority is moving towards widespread regulation (2022).

They are a way of raising finance by asking many people each for a small amount of money. Traditionally, financing a business, project or venture involved asking a few people for large sums of money. Crowdfunding switches this idea around, using the internet to talk to thousands – if not millions – of potential funders. Typically, those seeking funds will set up a profile of their project on a website such as those run by our members. They can then use social media, alongside traditional networks of friends, family, and work acquaintances, to raise money.

Below is a brief description of each of the different type of crowdfunding.

Donation / Reward Crowdfunding

People invest simply because they believe in the cause. Rewards can be offered (often called reward crowdfunding), such as acknowledgements on an album cover, tickets to an event, regular news updates, free gifts and so on. Returns are considered intangible. Donors have a social or personal motivation for putting their money in and expect nothing back, except perhaps to feel good about helping the project.

UK Sites include:
www.fundit.buzz,
www.crowdfunder.co.uk,www.justgiving.com,
www.pleasefund.us

Debt Crowdfunding

Investors receive their money back with interest. Also called Peer-to-Peer (p2p) lending, (see below) it allows for the lending of money while bypassing traditional banks. Returns are financial, but investors also have the benefit of having contributed to the success of an idea they believe in. In the case of microfinance, where very small sums of money are leant to the very poor, most often in developing countries, no interest is paid on the loan and the lender is rewarded by doing social good.

Sites include:
www.abundanceinvestment.com
www.abundanceinvestment.com
www.fundingknight.com, www.trillionfund.com

Equity Crowdfunding

People invest in an opportunity in exchange for equity. Money is exchanged for a share, or a small stake in the business, project, or venture. As with other types of shares, apart from community shares, if it is successful the value goes up. If not, the value goes down. Sites include:

www.crowdcube.com, www.downingcrowd.co.uk, www.seedrs.com, www.propertypartner.co

How do you apply for a peer-to-peer loan?

To apply for a loan, go to one of the lending sites and register, select the amount you want to borrow and over what term. Then you can see if you'll qualify for a loan and the interest rate(s) you'll have to pay. Peer to peer lenders normally 'parcel up' the loans between lots of different people.

Depending on your credit rating and the individual platform, you might be offered less than you want to borrow, or you might be offered a certain amount at one interest rate and different rates of interest by other lenders.

Rules and regulations

Peer to peer platforms and some individual lenders, are, in most cases, regulated by the Financial Conduct Authority (FCA). That means that if you're unhappy and make a complaint, the business has eight weeks to sort it out. If, after eight weeks, you're still not happy, you can ask the Financial Ombudsman Service (FOS) to get involved. The FOS has official powers to sort out complaints between you and a financial business you're unhappy with. If they agree that the business has done something wrong, they can order them to put things right. The service is free to use.

Now read the key points from Chapter 8

**

Key points from Chapter 8

- Raising finance for a business can be difficult at the best of times. It can also be relatively easy depending on the viability of your business.

- Funding a business from your own resources, mortgaging property, borrowing from family and friends etc, is probably the safest and easiest way to obtain funds-of course this depends on availability

- There are several other areas of finance, the main one being banks-this is where a coherent business plan is necessary.

- Once started, other areas of finance can be trade credit, invoice factoring, hire purchase, Crowd Funding, Peer-to-Peer lending, lease agreements and so on. All these areas help with ongoing cash flow.

- There is a plethora of grants available from local and national government. European Union Grants are no longer available following BREXIT.

**

Ch. 9

Exercising Financial Control

In this chapter, we will consider the importance of financial control within the process of business planning. We will look at profit and loss forecasting, cashflow forecasting, effective bookkeeping, tax and insurance and raising capital for your business.

Profit and loss forecasting

A profit and loss forecast is a projection of what sales you think you will achieve, what costs you will incur in achieving those sales and what profit you will earn.

Having this information down on paper means that you will be able to refer to it and adjust it as your business develops. Not all the headings will be relevant to you, so don't worry if you leave blank spaces.

Cashflow forecast

A cashflow forecast, as the name suggests, forecasts the changes in the cash which comes into and out of your bank account each month. For example, your customers may pay you after one month, whereas you might pay out for rent or insurance in advance. At the same time, you will have to pay for certain costs such as materials or wages and will need to budget for this.

Preparing a Cashflow Forecast

Remember that a cashflow forecast helps you to evaluate the timing of money coming into and going out of your business. In showing you the "movement" of money, it takes full account of the fact that you may often not be paid immediately for work done and, correspondingly, that you may not have to pay immediately for goods and services you acquire.

An important purpose of a cashflow forecast is to reveal the gap between your cash receipts and payments. It will show you whether, for example, you might need to borrow, and if so, when you are most likely to require additional funds. It is very common for businesses to need more cash as they grow because of the difference in timing of receipts and payments.

Other Terms

Working Capital

Working capital is the term often used to describe the short-term resources used by the business for everyday trading purposes. This consists of:

Debtors-these are customers you have sold to in credit, i.e., they owe you money.

Creditors-these are your suppliers who you have purchased from on credit, i.e., you owe them money.

Stock-this represents the value of materials you have purchased. They may be purchased for immediate resale, or they may be in the process of being converted into a finished article.

Cash-this can either be the amount of physical cash you are holding, or it may be money held in a current or bank deposit account.

All the above have to be carefully controlled if your business is to prosper.

Over trading

A problem common to many small and growing businesses is what is described as "over trading". The more sales you make, the more money you will need to spend on funding material and debtors before you are paid for the sales. If your level of sales becomes too high and you do not have the necessary level of working capital to support it, you may simply run out of cash. This can be disastrous for your business and means that a full order book is not the only thing to strive for.

Even with a profitable business and a full order book, it is imperative to have enough cash available. Extra finance can help your cashflow and make it easier to avoid the pitfalls of over trading.

Collecting money on time

For every day a customer delays payments, your profit margin is eroded. You may have to pay interest charges on a loan or overdraft, when the money owed to you could be earning you interest instead.

Check your customer's ability to pay

Before you offer customers credit, check that they can meet their liabilities. You may want to take up bank references.

Set out your terms of trading

Be specific about when you expect payment, for example, 30 days from the date of the invoice and make your customer aware in advance of work that you do.

Set up a system

Set up a system which enables you to issue invoices promptly and shows you when invoices become overdue.

Keep clear and accurate records

Inaccurate invoices or unclear records can be one of the main reasons for customers delaying payments. Make sure you send invoices punctually, to the right person at the right address.

Collect your payment on time

Establish a collections routine and stick to it. Keep records of all correspondence and conversations. Give priority to your larger accounts but chase smaller amounts too. If regular chasing does not produce results, consider stopping further supplies to the customer. If payment is not obtained, don't hesitate to ask a reputable debt collection agency or solicitor to collect the money for you. Your Business activities will consist of selling goods and/or services. At the same time, you will have to spend money on behalf of the business, on the purchase or rent of premises, raw materials, equipment, stationery etc. to conduct business.

Remember that every business transaction generates a financial transaction, all of which must be recorded in books of account on an on-going basis. It is a fundamental management requirement that this be done on a regular basis, at a minimum once a week. Leave it much longer, and sooner or later an iron law of accounting will come into operation. You will have mislaid a financial record or simply forgotten to request one or issue one. When you do get around to updating the books, they won't balance. Unless you can discover the error before the end of the financial year your accountant will be faced with the task of reconciling "incomplete records", which he or she will enjoy because of the professional challenge but which costs you more money for more of his/her time.

What information must be kept?

As a minimum you must keep records of the following: -

i) All the invoices raised (or rendered) on behalf of the business, either when the goods are delivered or the services supplied, or shortly afterwards. An invoice is a legal document and constitutes a formal demand for money. It must provide enough information to identify the business which sent it, who it was sent to, what it is for and whether VAT is payable.

ii) A list of your Sales invoices numbered sequentially.

iii) All Purchase invoices received, and listed i.e., those demands made on your business for the payment of money.

iv) Wages and salaries paid, and to whom; Income tax and NI contributions paid over to the Tax authorities.

v) All chequebook stubs, paying-in slips/books, counterfoils of petty cash vouchers, business bank account statements. Without these you cannot compile your books of account.

vi) A full record of VAT, whether paid by or paid to the business.

The advantages of a bookkeeping system for your business

a) To provide accurate information sufficient to assess whether you are managing the business at a profit or a loss, or whether the business is solvent i.e., is there enough cash available in the business to pay all the outstanding liabilities on demand? The right information of the right kind at the right time is a vital management tool. Good management means making informed decisions of the right kind at the right time based on information that is true and therefore trustworthy.

b) To provide the information required for correct assessments of VAT and Income Tax, to avoid financial penalties (and possibly a suspect reputation) for incorrect and/or late payments. HMRC keep records for seven years, and so must you. Your accountant will need the best information to minimise your tax liabilities, unless of course you decide to submit a statement of income to your Inspector of Taxes without recourse to an accountant. In any event the Inspector will require a calculation of your Income from the business in the form of an Income and Expenditure Account for each trading year.

c) To monitor the behaviour of the business over time by reference to financial summaries "at a glance". You don't need to remember for example how many meals were served in your restaurant business say in this year compared with last year.

The comparison that matters is the financial one with reference to the value of those transactions.

How to record the information you need

There are basically four methods of bookkeeping. Which one to choose will depend largely on the type and size of business you have established. Take advice from a business adviser or accountant if you are unsure as to which is the best one for your needs.

a) Proprietary systems.

These are best suited for sole traders in cash transaction types of business e.g., jobbing builders, market traders or some small shopkeepers. This type of business requires daily record keeping, often including till-rolls for the cash till and offers a simple method of control over finances. Several pre-printed stationery systems are available at business bookshops. Select one that allows you enough space to record all that needs recording. Worked examples are set out at the beginning of each book to show you how to keep cash records and the bank position, which can be calculated by following the instructions included.

Cash businesses are more vulnerable than other types for the following reasons: -

i) It is far easier to lose or misplace paperwork. Therefore, it is easier to lose control and lose money. Therefore, it is more difficult to plan.

ii) It is far more difficult to separate the cash that belongs in the business from the cash belonging to the proprietor.

iii) HMRC pay far closer attention to cash businesses because of the greater scope for "creative accounting" and tax evasion.

To minimise these risks, cash business-proprietors are strongly advised to pay their daily cash takings into the bank by using pre-printed paying-in books supplied by their bank. It is also vital to obtain receipts for purchases made from the takings and to keep them in an orderly fashion.

b) The Analysed Cash Book System.

This is perhaps the most common method used by small businesses selling mostly on credit, with perhaps some cash sales. It relies on the Single-Entry system of bookkeeping, where each entry is, as the name implies, made once only, and all entries are made in one book, the cashbook. The analysed cashbook is the "bible" of the business. It allows "at a glance" analysis because it is arranged on a columnar basis, showing how much has been received into the business, when and from where, how much of each receipt is attributable to VAT and therefore how much is the net amount belonging to the business. All this information is written up on one side of a pre-printed book, the left-hand page, showing all monies paid into the bank on behalf of the business. On the opposite, right-hand page is set out in separate columns details of what has been spent by the business, in other words, monies paid out of the bank, to whom and when.

See overleaf for example of the analysed cashbook.

The analysed cash book

Figure 1: Receipts side of an analysed cash book

ANALYSED CASH BOOK

Date	Details	Receipt number	Receipts Amount	Balance b/f	Sale of	Other
1 Jan	Cash in hand	-	1000.00	1000.00		
3 Jan	Grant from donor	500	9500 00			
9 Jan	Grant from Dept. of Health	501	7000.00			
9 Jan	Sale of drugs	502	14.50		14.50	
31 Jan	Total		17514.5	1000.00	14.50	-

See fig 2 overleaf for payments side.

Figure 2: Payments side of an analysed cash book

				ANALYSED CASH BOOK					
					Payments				
Date	Details	Receipt number	Amount	Salaries	Rent	Elect	Other expenses	Other	
3 Jan	Stationery for office	1	10.00				10.00		
5 Jan	Purchase of medical supplies	2	650.00						
7 Jan	Driver's salary	3	200.00	200.00					
7 Jan	Purchase of drugs	4	3450.00						
31 Jan	Total		4310.00	200.00	-	-	10.00		

c) The System of Double Entry

This method of recording accounts relies on ledgers, or separate books of account for each type of transaction. Far greater detail and control are possible using this system. As well as a cash account there is scope for setting up other ledgers such as the bought ledger for purchases, sales ledger, nominal (or business expense) ledger, salaries and so on. It is much easier to monitor how much has been spent over a period on each type of transaction, simply by referring to the ledger or account, on each of which a running balance is struck. Every transaction is recorded in the major account called the Cash Account and in the appropriate subsidiary ledger. In this way the Cash Account acts as a "Control" account for all the separate accounts of the business. The most important feature of this system is the characterisation of all bookkeeping entries as either a "credit" ("he trusts" i.e.," the business owes him") or "debit" ("he owes").

The sophistication of this method lies in the use of two entries for each transaction. For each credit entry in the Cash Account there must be a corresponding debit entry for the same amount in a different account. Likewise for each debit entry in the Cash Account there must be a corresponding credit entry in a different account. The key words are "equal and opposite". That way the greatest possible degree of control is obtained.

d) Computerised Accounting Systems

A wide variety of off-the-shelf packages are available, which rely on single or double entry methods. It may be tempting to invest in an accounts package at the outset, especially if you intend to use other computer packages in the business. It would be most unwise to start using such a package without understanding the principles that underlie them.

Businesses have failed because of the familiar - "GIGO" - garbage in, garbage out. Money is the lifeblood of the business so don't turn it into garbage by neglecting an understanding of what, why and how of bookkeeping.

Key points from chapter 9

- A profit and loss forecast are a projection of what sales you think you will achieve.

- A cashflow forecast forecasts the changes in the cash which comes into and out of your bank account each month.

- It is vital to understand the principle and practice of over trading.

- You need to keep clear and accurate records at all times.

- You should fully understand the basic principles of bookkeeping.

****

SECTION 5

ONLINE BUSINESSES-ADDITIONAL CONSIDERATIONS

Ch.10

Business Plans and Online Business-Additional Factors

In the following chapters, we will look specifically at online business and the factors that need to be looked at and then incorporated into a business plan. All the factors that have been covered relating to traditional businesses are relevant to online businesses.

The only major difference is the platform through which you intend to sell products and the way you reach consumers.

As mentioned in the introduction, without a doubt, the ascendancy of online businesses has taken the business world by storm over the last ten years or so. Indeed, up until recently (2022) more and more people were purchasing their goods online, to the overall detriment of the high street.

During the pandemic, the only businesses doing well were the online businesses. Because of the lockdowns in place, people were resorting to buying online as, quite simply they could not get out. However, as the lockdowns have disappeared, people are once again venturing out to the high street and online businesses are suffering. Just look at the share price of the technology companies.

Online businesses can still work, but now the emphasis is on what products you are selling and by successful planning at the outset.

The absolute key to any online business, as it is with any type of business, online or not, is the development of a clear and straightforward plan, one that will carry you through all the steps from inception to completion. The identification of your business, what it is you are supplying, goods or services and how you are going to supply them, how you are going to finance the business and how you are going to get paid, this is the bread and butter and must be clear at the outset.

You also need to remember that your online business, because it is web based, will cross boundaries, and may not necessarily be restricted to the UK. This will depend very much on what you are offering for sale.

Online v traditional business

There are several advantages to setting up an online business as opposed to a traditional business:

- Online is relatively inexpensive to create and maintain a presence
- There is an opportunity, because of the worldwide nature of the web, to attract a wider audience and a geographically targeted audience.

The technical side

As an online business, your web presence is of vital importance. This requires creating and maintaining the site and involves front-end development, i.e. creating the shop front online, database development, systems administration and general administration.

You, or someone that you are working with, will require the skills to maintain the shopping portal, the website. If you don't have the requisite skills, then you will need to hire them in. This costs money so it is vitally important that you have a clear brief for the experts to work from. It is also vitally important that you own the final product and remain in control. In short, develop a clear and unambiguous relationship with the web designers and systems administrators. If you get the design of your site wrong and it doesn't attract customers, then there is no real future. The technical aspects of setting up an online business are discussed in more depth in Section two.

The legal aspects of an online business

As with every operation there are legal implications for you and your business. This impacts on what you sell and where you sell it. You should seek legal advice when embarking on an online business, as although the law may appear straightforward it sometimes isn't.

As a bare minimum you need to display website terms and conditions and your privacy policy. If you intend to sell products outside of the United Kingdom then you need to be aware of any government restrictions, by the way of embargoes and any licenses you may need depending on territories that you want to sell in, particularly in relation to consumer electronics and entertainment or media products. Don't just go entering these markets without researching requirements.

Business operations, the supply chain and how you distribute your goods

One important area that needs to be examined is that of sourcing the goods that you intend to sell, (if you intend to sell physical goods as opposed to services) pricing those goods correctly and storage and ultimate distribution of those goods to their destination. You need to delve into the minutiae here and look at time frames for delivery of the goods to you, the basic costs of those goods, the storage of those goods and the costs of that storage and finally the delivery to the customer. Your initial pricing will reflect all these elements plus the amount for profit.

The managing of customer expectations and relationships

Finally, we come to one of the most important aspects of business, in particular online businesses, one which is quite often not considered until things go wrong, that is dealing with the customer, the person or organization that buys your product and makes a success of your business or otherwise.

Setting up Your Business Online

Your website is your shop window to the world. It goes without saying that this is one of the most important elements of an online business. If you don't have the technical expertise to create your own website, and most people don't, then you will need to have a very clear idea of what it is you are trying to create and find someone to work with. You will also have to have a clear idea of what your initial budget is for your website.

There are certain questions that you need to ask, such as:
- Do you know what it is that you require from your website?
- How many products will you be offering?
- What will be the ongoing maintenance requirements of the site?
- Will you want to regularly change the appearance of the site?
- Who exactly are you trying to target with your site?
- Website developers won't really be interested in your longer-term business plan but will require a well worked out brief. It is

essential that you look at websites selling similar content so you can get an idea of what it is you are trying to achieve.

- As a start you should write down the following:
- How many pages will your site require? In the first instance you don't need to worry about the pages that display products as these will be dynamically created as the site is developed. Of more importance is the number of static pages, such as 'contact us' 'about us' privacy policy and so on. When you have identified the static pages, you are well on the way to creating an initial sitemap.
- Note down the content and structure of the site, what is it that your site will contain, is it just text and images or will there be downloads, video clips and review sections etc.? By identifying this you will assist the developer in deciding on the most suitable technology for the site.
- Future content management. Who will do this in the future and how often will it need to be modified?
- Marketing. You will need to have an idea of which on and offline marketing channels you plan to use in conjunction with the business, so your developer can build in the functionality at the outset to allow this to happen in the future.
- Website monitoring. You will almost certainly want to know how well your site is performing in terms of number of visitors and sales. You will also want to know where the traffic is coming from. Make allowances to integrate tools such as Google Analytics into the site. If you are planning an e-commerce store, you will want more detailed financial reporting, not only basic sales information but also tools to manage returns, stock levels, VAT and so on.

Choosing a web developer

It's true to say that there are now literally thousands of website developers around, ranging from those with very little knowledge, they may have completed a basic course, to the more technically proficient and experienced. It is therefore vitally important, given the importance of getting it right at the outset, to carry out research on several developers. You will want to look carefully at the areas listed below.

Experience

You will want to assess how long the developer has been operating and what their track record is, what they have developed in the past. It would be a wise move to choose a developer who has had experience of developing websites for similar companies and therefore knows the requirements. An experienced developer will be able to discuss various technology options with you and the good and bad points associated with each.

Development skills and knowledge

It is likely that the developer that you are employing will have a far greater knowledge of web technology than you. However, you can ask such questions as-do they intend to build the website from scratch, or are they using an 'off the shelf' model, i.e., one that has been developed or partially developed for someone else?

If you are planning to sell products online then you will want to know their views on e-commerce/shopping basket solutions, whether they recommend PayPal or Worldpay for example (more about these later) can they set up a facility to pay by credit card and also will there be a basic content management system which will allow you or your staff to edit and delete items on the site without continuous recourse to the developer?

References from other clients

Any web developer worth his or her salt will not object to you asking other clients about the performance of the developer. As the investment in a website is one of the early major investments then it is of the utmost importance that some form of reference is taken up.

Future project management

You will want to ensure that the chosen developer explains how the process of developing the site works. You will need to ensure that it is brought in well within time and budget. Basic questions are how often you will be informed of progress, who your contacts are and how can they be reached. In addition, you will need to ascertain how flexible the developer is if you want to add or subtract a feature to the website halfway through development. There are other aspects of development that you need to take on board, such as where the developer is based, how accessible they are, what are their education and qualifications and, vitally, can you get on with them. You will have close contact with the developer, and you need to ensure that you have a good personal relationship with them. Communication is everything!

Payment methods over the web

There are several ways to facilitate payment over the web. The chosen method will need to be integrated by the designer. To enable online payment, you will need to set up a payment gateway and a merchant account. However, as we will see, there are several ways, some simpler than others, to set up a gateway. Payment gateways are an interface between your website, and the banks/card issuers around the world. There are many providers, and you can choose to work with a specialist provider or your own bank. Your own bank will invariably be happy to set up this gateway with you. You will need to look at the various methods on offer and compare the fees. Some charge more than others. Most providers will charge on a scale, meaning that the more transactions the cheaper it becomes. This may not be the best deal for a start up business, as your initial traffic and sales will be slow to build up. A merchant account is a depository into which funds you receive from online payments are made. This is one option. However, whichever option you choose, the process works as follows:

Step 1. Customer enters card details on your website.
Step 2. The card is authenticated-the details are sent via your payment gateway, to the card issuer. If the card details cannot be verified, then the card will be declined.
Step 3. Payment authorization-The issuing bank checks that the cardholder's details are correct and that there are enough funds to cover the transaction and that the card hasn't been reported lost or stolen. Once all checks are carried out then an instruction is sent to the bank to debit funds.
Step 4. Payment settlement-your account is credited within a few days of the actual transaction.

Arguably the most popular payment method which can easily be integrated into your site is PayPal. It provides a simple method for payment and the costs are low, particularly for a new business. There are other payment methods like PayPal which can be explored on the web.

The process of ordering

it is essential to ensure that once customers have chosen a

product or service then they can complete the ordering process, and that it is an easy path. I know from my own experience that a process that is too long-winded can work against the business and can lose you sales.

Ensure that the A-Z process is simple

Part of an integrated system for purchasing over a website is what is known as the 'shopping basket'. I am sure that you will have seen this on Amazon or similar sites. You are invited to place items in a shopping trolley before checkout. This gives the feeling that you are in an actual store. This is known as the order pipeline and is the process and the number of pages that a consumer must navigate before the completion of the sale. It is important that the order pipeline has as few stages as possible so that the customer doesn't become frustrated. Therefore, you need to define what details are essential to complete the order and what information can be captured later.

Supplying Goods and Services-The Supply Chain
Setting up your business and supplying goods and services

Given the current problems with sourcing and supplying the actual goods it is essential that you have a grasp of the problems inherent in supply chains. This is as relevant to online businesses as for traditional operations. The goods that you supply will be totally dependent on the type of business that you are running, whether you are selling actual physical goods or digital goods for example.

Local suppliers

If you are selling physical goods, if you can find a local supplier this will be a great advantage. The closer to home the supplier then the greater control that you will have. Local can mean anywhere within the UK. Local products mean reduced costs, lower freight charges, free local delivery or self-service pick up options. This will all help to save money. Also, local suppliers mean better stock management in that local suppliers can often hold onto stock until consignment.

Buying from abroad

Many products can be sourced cheaply from abroad, particularly from places such as China. Buying products from countries such as these will no doubt help to improve your profitability in the long run. However, unless you have the time to go to the relevant country and purchase goods, and you are fully aware of the tax implications, then all sorts of risks are presented.

Even if you cannot find the time or money to visit a potential trading partner abroad, there are many online trading platforms offering a huge range of suppliers and goods, (Business-to-Business platforms). Many charge businesses to advertise their contact details and place descriptions of their products, others will charge buyers a membership fee to gain access to contact details, some others charge a commission. A few such trading platforms are:

- www.alibaba.com
- www.tradekey.com
- www.globalsources.com
- www.diytrade.com

There are many more. Eventually you will want to meet suppliers and forge a relationship. There is nothing better than this to ensure confidence and security and to discuss trade terms.

Choosing a supplier of goods

You should keep all the data that you receive from the various potential suppliers. The name of the game is competition. For instance, when you have set up your business and are ready to go, you might eventually run into problems with your suppliers for a variety of reasons, price, service delivery, customer care and so on, and may want to switch supplier. You should build up a data bank of suppliers so that you are able to move if necessary.

Managing the suppliers

Maintaining good relations with your suppliers is as important as managing your customers. Suppliers are very important; without them you don't really have a business. Managing suppliers well is wholly dependent on how well you communicate with them. There are many instances of relationships starting off well and then something goes wrong and the whole pack of cards collapses. The essence of good management is face-to-face communication. Find time to meet on a regular basis with your suppliers. Remember they have their own pressures too, so sit down and talk about any problems that may arise. That goes a long way.

Organising payment terms

With a new business, it is highly unlikely that you will be given immediate credit by suppliers. Even if you are known personally to the supplier from a previous life, the first order will have to be paid up front.

However, once you have a history with a supplier, once you have maintained regular payments, then it is likely that you will be given time to pay. Usually, 30 days from invoice date is the norm. The same goes with your business bank account. In the first instance it is very unlikely that you will be given generous business overdraft terms. Again, it will be dependent on your track record. our relationship with a supplier begins from the word go when you place your first order. Make sure that the account information that they have is correct, the billing address, delivery address, contact numbers and email address, along with VAT number if applicable and payment terms.

When you receive an order be rigorous and check that the contents are what you ordered, and that the quantity is correct. Mistakes can happen and they should be rectified at the outset otherwise problems can arise.

Breaking off relationships with a supplier
No matter how good the relationship is with your supplier, there may come a time when you will need to sever ties. It may be that things started to go wrong, and they have progressively got worse. There could have been a change of personnel and the time and effort that has been expended building up a relationship has all gone out of the window. Whatever, it is time to switch.

Once you have found a replacement supplier then you will need to notify your existing supplier that you no longer require their services and that all outstanding invoices will be paid. Although feelings may have been hurt, business comes first. It is highly likely that you will have warned your supplier beforehand of problems so it may not come as a shock.

Stock control
The type of business that you run and the type of goods that you provide, will determine the level of stock control that will be required. If someone is ordering from you and you order the goods from someone else, and they are delivered direct to the buyer's door then the whole process of stock control is simple. However, if

you are buying goods in bulk at one price and delivering direct to the customer yourself then this will require a different system. To run your e-commerce store smoothly from the outset, you will need to make sure that you have the correct tools to do this.

Bar code printer
Depending on the type of products that you are planning to sell and how far up the supply chain you are sourcing your products, you will need to obtain a bar code printer. Bar codes make light work of stock management and a bar code printer will prove invaluable if you need to label your product.

Bar code scanners
To assist you in both receiving and picking and packing customer orders, a barcode scanner will be most useful. Setting up your back office will take time initially as you assign each product a bar code but once done then stock can move quickly into and out of the warehouse.

Stock management systems
In the first instance, a simple spreadsheet might suffice to keep accurate records of stock movement. However, as your business grows and becomes more complex it is likely that you will need a more sophisticated system. There are several systems around that might be suitable and if you require a demonstration, it is likely that a company would be willing to do this for you.

Invoicing customers
As we have seen in the previous chapter, controlling cash flow is the lifeblood of any business. Spending money is easy but getting the money in can be a different story. It is your legal obligation to

provide customers with an invoice and a receipt along with every order shipped. Invoices can detail numerous orders on one sheet. The invoice must contain basic details, such as your company address and your registration details plus VAT number if applicable. The customer's order must be fully outlined and the price that they have paid. Whilst all of this sounds obvious it is amazing how many companies send out inadequate invoices which are then not paid. In addition, it goes without saying that invoices must be tracked, and late payers contacted immediately. Strong credit control is vitally important. Again, it is amazing how many companies send out invoices then lose track of them doing nothing about them until they accidentally discover, or their accountant discovers, that they haven't been paid.

The storage of stock

If you are in a position where you must store stock before delivery, then there are a few basic rules that you should observe:

- Make sure that where you store your stock is appropriate-i.e., it is dry and clean and suits the goods that you plan to store. Any damage to goods once delivered from the original supplier to you will be down to you.
- Make sure that the storage is secure and protected from fire or theft-ensure adequate alarms and current insurance is in place
- Make sure that you have adequate systems in place to check goods received. If the incorrect number of goods arrives, or there is damage this should be dealt with then and there.
- Carry out regular stock takes. This becomes more important as the business grows.
- Make sure that stock is stored in a logical and ordered way. Have clearly numbered areas where specific stock resides so it can be found easily.

Picking and packing stock

In the first instance, the picking of stock may not be a great problem as your business will probably be small. However, it is when it grows that it can become more complex.

The following are tips for you when organising the selection of stock:

- You should have a picking list which enables you to go straight to the item you want. This will save time and effort
- Ensure that an invoice/receipt is sent with every order
- If you don't have all the items when packing the order notify the customer straight away
- Ensure items are well packaged to avoid damage

Delivery of items

This is always a contentious area. My own experience of delivery has been that no matter how much companies put into promoting the product and making all sorts of promises, the end link in the chain, delivery of items, lets them down. There is nothing worse than a surly delivery driver virtually throwing the goods at you or refusing to carry goods up the stairs or whatever. In short, rudeness and inflexibility. I hasten to add that this isn't true across the board, but it is in many cases. Given that everything about online shopping should be about convenience, including delivery, then it is important to choose the right partner, which could be Royal Mail, FedEx or any one of the delivery companies. Usually, you would sign a deal with one or other that can guarantee price and provide some sort of track record when it comes to delivery. Courier companies will usually offer attractive rates for volume deliveries so it will be up to you to negotiate the appropriate contract. You should look for the following:

- Courier companies who will collect from your address and can give specified times for delivery
- Some companies will also handle returns as part of the contract, make sure that this is in your contract
- International orders are slightly different-they must have a customs statement from your company clearly marked on the outside of the package that includes a description of the contents. You can check with www.hmrc.gov.uk for more information.

Returns

There are several reasons why returns are made: incorrect goods sent to the customer, damaged goods or customer changes his or her mind. Whatever the reason, returns happen and must be dealt with. The following are useful tips when dealing with returns:

- When the good is returned check the damage, if damage is alleged, to see whether this is down to you or to the manufacturer
- Make sure you keep an accurate record of returns and adjust stock accordingly
- Acknowledge that you have received the return-this is good customer service and might encourage the customer to buy again Keep an eye of people who buy and return on a regular basis-this can happen, especially with items such as DVD's, which can be copied. After a while you can sort out those who are operating this kind of scam.

****

Chapter 11

Creating Your Business Plan-The Finer Points

Although there is a lot of information to absorb, hopefully, the previous chapters have raised awareness of the many areas of business that you need to be aware of before putting together a clear (and convincing) business plan. The following pages represent the basis for your business plan and the various sections relate to the sections of the book. If there are parts which you do not feel are relevant to your business, then you should ignore them.

Business plans can be formulated by those already in business and wishing to expand, or by those who wish to obtain funds for a start up. The ideas gleaned from this book will assist people in formulating any type of business plan.

You should construct your own business plan using the outline below as a guide. By referring to the book and to the details of your own business you should be able to formulate your plan which will be the complete document for your use, particularly for presentation to your bank manager or to other parties. Remember, it has been stressed throughout the book that an impressive business plan goes a long way towards developing your business and raising the necessary funds to go forward.

Constructing the plan

If you have never written a business plan before, it can be difficult to tell exactly how to go about it. What kind of format should you use, is there an ideal length, how should you order the sections in the plan? There are a few main guidelines which should be followed.

Main considerations

- The language used must be concise and to the point. It should be written in layman's terms and in the third person.
- Each section must stand on its own and clearly define and satisfy its objective.
- All conclusions drawn from facts are to be reasonable and credible.
- Where appropriate, facts should be supported by graphs and charts as this makes the statement immediately more visual.

Presentation

- Choose the right font-don't for example couch the whole plan in a tiny font which people cannot read. The normal font for presentation is Times Roman 12.
- Use single spacing between lines.
- Make sure that it is well laid out with sub-headings
- Page numbering to be consistent-usually on bottom right-hand corner.
- Formatting on page numbers must be consistent.
- Bullet point marks must be used effectively.
- The plan should contain enough white space for readability.

Cover/Table of contents

The cover page should detail:
- The name of the business
- The main contact's name
- Full address details
- Type of company
- The clients company logo; and
- Reader confidentiality.

The table of contents should include the executive summary-what is in the plan and any appendices.

In the next chapter is an example of a basic business plan. You can use this as a model but will certainly need to adapt it how you wish, to suit your own business. You may find that some of the sections are not relevant, and it will also depend on who you are showing the plan to and for what purpose.

****

Ch. 12

An Example Business Plan Template

Example business plan

(Cover page)

Name of business

_____

Address

_____
_____

Contact name

_____

Telephone Number

_____

Sole Trade
Partnership
Franchise
Limited Company

Start up date

Type of Business

Online or traditional or both

1. Executive Summary of the plan

_____

_____

_____

_____

2. Planning ahead

My goal is:

_____

_____

_____

_____

I expect to achieve the following over the next few years

Year 1

_____

_____

Year 2

_____

_____

Year 3

_____

3. Marketing

I have identified my market as:

_____
_____
_____
_____
_____
_____
_____
_____

My customers may be described as

_____
_____
_____
_____
_____
_____
_____
_____
_____
_____

4. Product comparison table

_____
_____

Creating an Effective Business Plan-The Easyway

	My Product	Competitor A	Competitor B
Price			
Quality			
Availability			
Customers			
Staff Skills			
Reputation			
Advertising			
Delivery			
Location			
Special Offers			
After Sales Service			

My product is special because

5. The main advantages of my product over my competitors are

_____
_____
_____
_____
_____

6. Pricing

Calculating your break even point

Personal Drawings

_____
_____

National Insurance

_____
_____

Tax

_____
_____

Stationary

_____
_____

Advertising

_____

Telephone

___

Rent and Rates

___

Heating and Lighting

___

Vehicle Depreciation

___

___

Petrol

___

___

Servicing

___

___

Road Tax Fund

___

___

Insurance

___

___

Business Insurance

_____

Bad debts

_____

7. Premises

My business will be located at

_____
_____
_____
_____
_____

Because

_____
_____
_____
_____
_____

Details of my lease/licence/rent/rate/next rent review

_____
_____
_____

8. Details of key staff (if any)

Name
_____
_____

Position
_____
_____

Address
_____

Age
_____
_____

Qualifications
_____
_____
_____

Relevant work experience
_____
_____
_____
_____
_____

Present Income

_____

_____

I will need to buy in the following skills during the first two years

_____

_____

_____

_____

_____

9. I estimate the cost of employing people or buying any services I may need in (including web development) the first two years

Number of people	Job Function	Monthly Cost	Annual cost

My personal Details

Name
_____

Address

_____

_____

_____

_____

Telephone (home)

_____

Telephone (work)
_____
_____

Qualifications
_____
_____
_____
_____
_____

Date of Birth
_____
_____

Business experience
_____
_____
_____
_____
_____

Courses attended
_____
_____
_____
_____

_____
_____

10. Financial Control/Accounting

I intend to keep the following records
(Which will be kept up to date by myself/bookkeeper/accountant)

_____
_____

Other

Accountant

_____
_____

Address

_____
_____

Telephone

_____
_____

Solicitor

Address

_____
_____

_____

Telephone
_____

VAT Number
_____

Insurance Arrangements
_____

Raising finance

By reference to my profit and loss and cashflow forecast, I need to borrow

Amount £
_____

For
_____
_____

Period
_____
_____

I am investing £
_____

11. I can offer the following security

_____

_____

****

Ch.12

Tips on Buying an Existing Business

This book has centered around creating a new business and formulating a business plan around this. However, you may be in a position where you are thinking of buying an existing business. This chapter offers a few tips on what to look for when buying an existing business.

There are many businesses available for sale in all areas of the market and this is, sadly, an area where many people end up losing out, usually to people or concerns that are trying to offload a business that is failing.

Inspecting a business for sale
If you have identified a business that interests you, it will be necessary to make several visits to that business and to carry out several 'due diligence' checks. In addition to appraising the business from the standpoint of its operations, such as the flow of customers, attitude of the staff, premises, and stock, it is essential that you have a handle on the valuation of the business. Many times, business is overvalued and overstate their turnover. It is vital to involve professionals, such as lawyers and accountants at the outset. This may cost but is nothing compared to the cost to you if you buy a business and realise that it is failing.

There will be several elements involved in forming the price of a business, such as building and stock. It will be essential to ensure that a correct appraisal is carried out. Are the assets as valuable as they are said to be, i.e., their book value? Is the total turnover accurately stated and is it a realistic appraisal of ongoing year on year turnover? Where are the risks? You will also need to examine the following:

- Trade debtors
- Trade creditors
- Other creditors
- Any agreements such as hire purchase and leases, including leases on buildings
- Bank loans

Basically, you will need to ensure that you are not purchasing a risk and that all agreements in place will apply to you when you purchase a business.

Goodwill

There is usually an amount involved for 'goodwill' in a business. This will be the payment for having built up the business and their brand name and their commercial reputation.

Extreme care should be taken in this area. The owner will argue that they have spent years building up the business. The counter argument will be that benefits have been taken out of the businesses over the years THAT have been produced by the development of goodwill. A professional appraisal of this area is needed.

The process of purchasing a business

When you have been through the process of due diligence, it will be necessary to employ the services of a lawyer who specialises in the sale of commercial properties. This person will draw up a suitable contract of sale, compile a schedule of assets and liabilities that are to be included in the sale and the agreed valuation, search companies house for details of all existing directors and shareholders and other information and complete the necessary forms to register the transfer.

Although this chapter has been brief, the main message is BEWARE when buying a business and carry out a thorough investigation of what you are buying. Look out for any cover-ups and any likely future risks and make sure before you enter the purchase that you are totally committed.

****

CONCLUSION

The aim of this book is to ensure that, having read and understood all the key stages of business development, that you are now able to formulate an effective business plan. To many people, the very word 'business plan' makes them very nervous because it means work, often delving into areas that are beyond an individuals' control. If you go to a bank manager for a loan, he or she will always ask to see a business plan to gain the confidence to lend money. Without a business plan, to the bank manager at least, a person is proceeding in an unstructured way, often taking unacceptable risks, and cannot accurately forecast where the business will be in 6 months or one year's time.

It is hoped that having worked your way through the areas of business development and understood the model business plan laid out in chapter twelve, that you will find the process of planning that much easier. A word of advice: if you are in the process of starting up a business, always plan and plot a way forward that will enable you to see the coming year(s) very clearly. This will be of benefit to both yourself and those who you wish to get on your side in the future, be it a bank manager or government department.

If you are a business in the process of trading and need a plan, put aside time to do this, it is perhaps the most important element in the business process.

Good luck!

Useful Addresses

Advisory Conciliation and Arbitration Service (ACAS)
https://acas.org.uk
Tel 0300 123 1100

British Chambers of Commerce
65 Petty France
London SW1H 3QB
Tel 0207 654 5800
www.britishchambers.org.uk

British Franchising Association,
www.thebfa.org

Business in the Community
137 Shepherdess Walk (London Head Office)
London N1 7RQ
Tel 0207 7566 8650
www.bitc.org.uk
Also offices in Northern Ireland, Wales, and Scotland.

Business Links
See local phone books or
Small firms and business links
Division
www.businesslink.gov.uk

Department for Business, Energy and Industrial Strategy
1 Victoria Street
London
SW1H OET
020 7215 5000

The Chartered Institute of Patent Attorneys
2nd Floor, Halton House
20-23 High Holborn
London EC1N 2JD
020 7405 9450
www.cipa.org.uk

Companies Registration Office
Registrar of Companies (England and Wales)
Companies House
Crown Way
Cardiff
CF14 3UZ
DX 33050 Cardiff
Emailenquiries@companies-house.gov.uk
Enquiries (UK) 0303 123 4500
Welsh service welshcoordinator@companieshouse.gov.uk
International +44 303 1234 500

The Cardiff office is open 24 hours a day for the receipt of documents
Contact Centre lines are open between 8.30am to 6pm (Monday to Friday)

Registrar of Companies (Northern Ireland)

Companies House
2nd Floor
The Linenhall
32-38 Linenhall Street
Belfast
BT2 8BG
DX481 N.R. Belfast 1
Emailenquiries@companies-house.gov.uk
Enquiries (UK) 0303 1234 500
International +44 303 1234 500
Opening hours between 9am to 5pm (Monday to Friday)
The office does not have a letterbox for deliveries

Registrar of Companies (Scotland)

Companies House
4th Floor
Edinburgh Quay 2
139 Fountainbridge
Edinburgh
EH3 9FF
LP - 4 Edinburgh 2 (Legal Post) or DX ED235 Edinburgh 1
Emailenquiries@companies-house.gov.uk
Enquiries (UK) 0303 1234 500
International +44 303 1234 500
Opening hours between 9am to 5pm (Monday to Friday)
The Edinburgh office has a letterbox for out of hours deliveries

London office and information centre
Companies House
4 Abbey Orchard Street
Westminster
London
SW1P 2HT
Emailenquiries@companies-house.gov.uk
Enquiries (UK) 0303 1234 500
International +44 303 1234 500
Opening hours between 9am to 5pm (Monday to Friday)
The London office has a letterbox for out of hours deliveries

Confederation of British Industry (CBI)
Cannon Place
78 Canon Street
London EC4N 6HN
Tel 0207 379 7400
www.cbi.org.uk

Forum of Private Business
2 – 3 Ashley Hall, Ashley Hall Showground, Ashley, Cheshire, WA14 3QA
01565 626 001
info@fpb.org
www.fpb.org

Health and Safety Executive
hse.gov.uk

Federation of Small Businesses
Sir Frank Whitttle Way
Blackpool Business park
FY4 2FE
Tel 0808 20 20 888

Scottish Enterprise
Atrium Court
50 Waterloo Street
Glasgow G2 6HQ
Tel 0300 013 3385

Websites

National Enterprise Network
www.nationalenterpriseetwork.org

National Business Register
www.start.biz

The Princes Trust
www.princes-trust.org.uk

****

Index

Advertising, 6, 65, 67, 82, 136, 137
Affiliation, 74
Agents, 68, 154
Amazon, 77, 121
Analysed Cash book System, 106
Auditing resources, 4, 31

Bar code printer, 9, 125
Bar code scanners, 9, 125
Blogging, 77
BREXIT, 11, 98
Budgeting, 19
Business, 3, 4, 7, 9, 10, 11, 18, 21, 23, 27, 35, 37, 42, 43, 82,
    91, 93, 94, 102, 129, 133, 142, 147, 153,
    154, 156, 157
Business control systems, 35
Business loans, 91

Capital funding, 18
Cash flow, 19
Cashflow forecast, 7
Chartered Institute of Patent Agents, 44
China, 122
Competitors, 7, 83
Computerised Accounting Systems, 109
Constructing the plan, 130
Contract hire, 7, 92
Contributions Agency Office, 53
Co-registration, 76
Costs, 81
Creditors, 100
Customer expectations, 8, 116

Daltons Weekly, 43
Database development, 114

Debtors, 100
Department for Business innovation and Skills, 94
Department for Employment and Learning, 94
Department for Environment, Food and Rural Affairs, 94
Direct mail, 6, 68
Directories, 6, 66

Ebay, 77
Economic, 3, 30, 31
Email marketing, 74
Employment agencies, 55
Enterprise Agencies, 93, 157
Enterprise Ireland, 94
Environment, 30, 94
Evaluation of future options, 4, 32
Executive summary, 24

Facebook, 76
Factoring, 7, 90
Finance leases, 92
Financial performance, 35
Financial resources, 4, 32
Franchises, 4, 41
Front-end development, 114

Goodwill, 10, 148
Grants, 7, 93, 94

Her Majesty's Revenue and Customs, 39
Hire purchase, 7, 91
Human resource analysis, 35
Human resources, 4, 32

Inspecting a business for sale, 147
Intellectual property, 44
Internet marketing, 69
Investment franchises, 44

Investment of own funds, 89
Invoice discounting, 7, 90

Job centres, 5, 55
Job franchise, 43

Large businesses, 19
Leaflets, 6, 65
Legal requirements, 18
Local Authority inspectors, 50
Local suppliers, 9, 121
Location, 5, 19, 47, 57, 136
Long-term finance, 7, 91

Magazines, 66, 67
Management, 4, 18, 33, 34
Managing customers, 113
Marketing, 5, 64, 79, 113, 117
Mission statements, 3, 28, 29, 37

National government, 94
National Insurance, 5, 52, 53, 82, 137
National Insurance Contributions, 5, 52, 53
Networking, 42
Newspaper advertising, 6

Objectives, 3, 27
Online businesses, 11, 113, 116, 121
Operating lease, 92
Over trading, 7

Pandemic, 11
Partnerships, 4
Patents, 4, 44
Payment gateways, 119
Payment methods, 9, 119
PayPal, 118, 120

Personnel, 18
PESTE analysis, 30, 37
Physical resource analysis, 35
Physical resources, 4, 32
Planning, 4, 5, 33, 34, 49, 134
Planning and allocation of resources, 33, 34
Political, 3, 30
Presentation, 9, 130
Price, 18, 136
Pricing, 6, 81
Profit and loss forecasting, 7
Profits, 84
Proprietary systems, 8, 105
Publicity, 42

Quality, 18, 136

Radio advertising, 6
Raising finance, 7, 89, 98, 144
Recruiting, 5, 55
Returns, 9, 128
Rich media, 76

Sales representatives, 68
Search engine optimization, 70
Search Engine Results Pages, 70, 72
Shareholders, 40, 41
Short term finance, 90
Short-term finance, 7
Short-term objectives, 27
SMART, 3, 27, 28, 29, 37
Social, 4, 30, 31, 76
Soft loans, 7, 93
Stock, 100
Stock control, 9, 124
Stock management systems, 9, 125
Strategic analysis, 3, 30

Strategic implementation, 4, 33
Strategic management, 29
Strategic threats, 4, 35
Supply chain, 8, 115
System Double Entry, 108
Systems administration, 114

Tax, 5, 52, 82, 103, 104, 137, 138
Technological, 4, 30, 31
Television, 6, 67
Trade credit, 7, 90
Trademarks, 4
Training, 5, 55
Twitter, 76

Ukraine, 11
United Kingdom, 115

Web presence, 114
Welsh Development Agency, 94
Working from home, 5
Writing your plan, 3, 23

****